INBOX DETOX

AND THE HABIT OF E-MAIL EXCELLENCE

MARSHA EGAN

INBOX DETOX
AND THE HABIT OF E-MAIL EXCELLENCE

ISBN: 978-0-9815589-8-1

Library of Congress
TK5105.73 .E32 2008 004.692

To my husband, Bob.

Table of Contents

hab·it [hab-it] – noun

1. an acquired behavior pattern regularly followed until it has become almost involuntary: the habit of looking both ways before crossing the street.

Dictionary.com Unabridged (v 1.1). Random House, Inc. 01 May. 2008

Preface

In February of 2007, after Reuters released the article, "Are you an e-mail addict? There is an Executive Coach from Pennsylvania with a 12-Step Program," featuring my 12 Steps to controlling your inbox and your e-mail, bloggers all over the world had a field day with Step 5— Empty Your Inbox.

Their responses were, "Sure — I'd love to empty my inbox — what year will that happen???!", "Easier said than done!", and "What is she smoking? That's what we all want to do!"

At first I didn't understand their disagreement with and degradation of the step. After all, it made sense to me — move things out of your inbox so you can manage your work! Then I realized that those who were taking issue must have been plagued with the same challenge as many people who suffer under their e-mail—they use their inboxes as reminders, holding tanks, task managers, or just a place where e-mails collect. They had interpreted emptying their inboxes with *finishing* all their work, instead of managing it.

It became clear to me then that the key to successful e-mail management is not about just working or handling your e-mail, but much more about shifting your habits.

And mostly about changing yourself. And that is what is NOT being said by the thousands of people offering solutions to people crying e-mail overload.

And *that* is why this book is different. You can't just read this book and be instantly "cured," just like you can't read a diet book and be instantly thin. Like the person who wants to lose 100 pounds, the solution may be simple to understand, but the change of habit can be much more challenging, yet much more rewarding.

So—detoxifying your inbox is NOT a one-time fix. It requires ingraining new habits.

This book is your motivation for that habit shift. Inbox Detox is your guide to learning the absolutely most efficient ways of handling your e-mail, then changing your habits so that they become ingrained and second nature to you. It takes time and focus to change habits, and that habit-shift leads to maintaining an empty inbox, every time you open it. An empty inbox is not a symptom or even a result. It is evidence that you've taken healthy control of your e-mail... and your life.

Isn't that what we all want?

PART I

THE DETOX

THE EXASPERATION

Chances are, you've thought or said one or more of these stress laden comments:

"I have over 3000 items in my inbox. No matter how I try to stay ahead, it is beating me down. It is a never ending battle."

"I hate mornings—opening my e-mail with all those messages in my inbox defeats me before I have my first cup of coffee."

"I almost don't want to go on vacation—I don't want to have to deal with those hundreds of e-mails when I return!"

"My inbox is an endless source of stress."

"How do I stop friends from sending me daily jokes without losing them as friends???!"

"If I get one more inspirational e-mail telling me that if I don't forward it in 20 seconds, I'll live in purgatory, I'll scream!"

"My e-mail must multiply overnight as I sleep!"

"Why in the world did I get a copy of THAT message???!"

"Lucky me, my boss catches up on his e-mail over the weekend. I can count on at least 25 e-mails from him Monday morning. No wonder I hate Mondays!"

"I have so many items in my inbox, I find myself just starring at it — A LOT!"

These are symptoms that your inbox has become toxic to you. You're ready for the detox.

THE CHARACTERS

A nd not only is your inbox a source of toxic stress, the e-mailers around you are too!

Everyone has tales of stupid stuff others do with their e-mail. Stuff that aggravates them so much that they go on and on and on about it. You know what and who we're talking about! These people's nasty habits are infectious...

Throughout this book, you'll meet several of these toxic e-mailers. Some of their habits are so excessive, they take on a humorous side. We've even given them names that reflect their habits. You'll "meet" them when you see this:

So as to not continue to just frustrate you by reminding you of those people infecting our lives, we've also suggested the "antidote" for each toxic e-mailing annoyance as part of the alert.

Let's see if you know any of these people... Or, dig deep-
-does this description fit you? If so, you've got work to do.

Let's meet our first toxic e-mailer:

Toxic E-mailer Alert

E-COWARD ETHAN

E-coward Ethan is the person who "hides" behind e-mail, and actually takes stronger or more controversial positions when e-mailing rather than when in person.

I worked with a person who was what some might call a "people pleaser." He was always agreeable, and whenever he was approached on issues, was almost overly accommodating. Dr. Jekyll turned into Mr. Hyde when he hit the keyboard: He not only said "no" more often, but did so in terse, almost unkind ways. He also used e-mail to corner people when he thought they made mistakes, something he never did in person. This seemingly dual personality ultimately resulted in a lack of trust, and created real challenges for him in gaining collaboration and results.

Ethan's Antidote: *Don't do it! Be courageous in person, not by e-mail. With so much of the communication filters lost in e-mail communications, e-mail can add even more confusion, stress and controversy to the business commerce in the operation.*

THE EVOLUTION

Before we get into your detox program, we want to make sure you have some context for your remedy.

To embrace the cure for toxic e-mail behavior, let's understand how it started. How has e-mail overload so pervasively affected people throughout the world? How did it grow so fast? And why didn't we see it coming?

E-mail misuse hasn't always been pervasive in business. When workers first started using e-mail, although it was very cutting edge, most people used it sensibly—checking only when it was convenient, and in conjunction with other important methods of communicating pertinent information. People received only a few e-mails a week. Then customers began e-mailing multiple times a day, which required a response in an effort to deliver excellent customer service. In the middle of this, AOL and Yahoo enabled easy and inexpensive personal e-mail. The more e-mail was sent, the more was received. Then e-mailers discovered group lists. People started to use e-mail instead of the phone. As people became increasingly comfortable with it, they used e-mail more and more.

> # E-mail misuse hasn't always been pervasive in business.

It began in 1968, when the firm Bolt Beranek and Newman (BBN) was hired by the United States Defense Department to create the ARPANET (Advanced Research Projects Agency Network), which later became the Internet. Its purpose was to create a method by which military and educational institutions could communicate with each other. As part of this, in 1971, engineer Ray Tomlinson developed a method that allowed users on the same machine to send messages to each other. Tomlinson also put his mark on history by introducing the "@" sign to show that the intended recipient was "at" a host different from the local host.

One of the first e-mail programs available to the general public was Eudora, authored in 1988 by Steve Dorner. It was supplanted several years later by Netscape and Internet Explorer, which offered free e-mail service with a web browser. Then, in 1993, the large network service providers America Online and Delphi connected their proprietary e-mail systems to the Internet, beginning large-scale adoption of Internet e-mail as a global standard.

Gradually, the staple of e-mail entered the business culture, giving workers a new communication tool. It was efficient, fast, effective, and inexpensive. E-mail now has become something employees can't work without—ever—

and something that a business-person should value to ensure he or she does not miss anything.

When e-mail first came to the business world, people received one or two e-mails in a day. Managers and executives didn't even consider any productivity losses attributable to e-mail misuse—it was more commonly viewed as a productivity enhancer.

In fact, one of my corporate projects in the mid 80s was to develop a major campaign to encourage the use of e-mail among our 20,000 employees. We came up with a caricature of "the E-Male," a funny-looking super-hero type with a big E on his chest. The slogan read, "Have you E-mailed today?"

Though businesses were quick to adopt this efficient new system of communication, e-mail use amounted to just a fraction of what it has become today. Ferris Research International estimated the number of e-mail users in 2007 at around 780 million. Ferris also estimated the typical number of e-mails sent and received by a business user at about 600 per week.[1] In August 2008, the Radicati Group estimated the number of e-mails sent per day to be around 210 billion.

E-mail has undergone unprecedented growth. Yet, the incredible escalation of e-mail as a preferred method of communication snuck up on the business and social

---

1 Ferris Research, *The Email Security Market, 2005-2010,* http://www.ferris.com/?p=310118 Radicati Group (Aug 2008), http://email.about.com/od/emailtrivia/f/emails_per_day.htm

11

> # The incredible escalation of e-mail snuck up on the business and social world.

world. No one could have anticipated how rapidly it would permeate business culture or predicted its influence on the global economy.

"E-mail overload gives many workers the sense that their work is never done," according to senior analyst David Ferris, whose firm Ferris Research said there were 6 trillion business e-mails sent in 2006, according to *The Washington Post* in May of 2007.[2]

Looking back at the relatively modest rate of e-mail usage in the mid-90s, it is understandable that employers did not pay much attention to or implement efficient e-mail practices right away. The growth was so gradual that the amount of e-mail workers received was spread out enough to mask the outbreak of wide-scale productivity drain for businesses and individuals.

A good analogy to the slow growth of devastating e-mail practices is the parable of the frog — he jumped into a pot of water sitting on a campfire, and remained comfortable as the temperature of the water increased. The frog ultimately boiled himself to death because he

---

2 Mike Musgrove, *"E-mail Reply to All: Leave Me Alone," The Washington Post*, May 25, 2007

failed to notice the gradual change in the temperature until it was too late. Had he jumped into the pot when it was boiling, he would have immediately jumped out.

Likewise, the spread of e-mail snuck up on the business community. The global workforce experienced a gradual invasion of e-mail messages that required action. Had employers anticipated the drain on business productivity, they may have been better equipped to manage the growth before it infected the workforce. Companies might have developed proactive measures in the form of efficient and effective e-mail guidelines and best practice standards. Instead, people were left to develop their own e-mail habits through repetition and "infection." The multitude of e-mail messages received by workers each day influence their e-mail handling habits.

THE SEDUCTION

But e-mail has a dark side, the side that seduces individuals into ingraining habits that sap their energy and their lives. This is the dark side that is silently draining profits, adding stress, and diminishing business and personal productivity among office workers, from the boardroom to the mailroom. Employees compulsively check their business and personal inboxes throughout the workday, resulting in a staggering decline in worker productivity. For some, this seduction has become an obsession. Time wasted is money lost, and few companies can afford the strain on productivity that e-mail misuse can stimulate if it is ignored.

While companies are losing worker productivity, employees are extending the length of their workdays, going to the office on weekends, and checking their e-mail while on vacation because they can no longer manage the volume of communication that requires their attention. This is how e-mail habits have become toxic to individuals and businesses alike.

E-mail misuse is not just a crisis, it is an epidemic—a

worldwide infection that begins at an individual level. Employees are regularly using inefficient practices to handle their daily communications that, through repeated application, become habits. These unhealthy habits, multiplied by the ever-increasing amount of e-mail received, turn this wonderful timesaving tool into an incredible drain on a company's output. These bad habits then infect coworkers. E-mail mismanagement rapidly spreads throughout the organization and ultimately culminates in staggering loss of productivity for the employer. With the speed and pervasiveness of e-mail, more and more people's e-mailing habits have become toxic. This translates into millions of dollars of lost profits for businesses everyday, all over the globe.

> # The cost to both individuals and to business is astronomical.

Wide-spread unhealthy e-mail use results in a staggering loss in employee effectiveness, yet goes undiscussed in the boardroom even though it is likely the number-one cost factor draining the productivity of global business.

With the huge impact on workplace efficiency, you might ask, "Why didn't we see it coming?"

There are two reasons.

First, the productivity loss happens in very small chunks

of time. When employees check e-mail compulsively, they aren't just wasting the time it takes them to read the newly received message. There is an ancillary cost. It is commonly accepted that it takes employees a minimum average of four minutes to recover from each workplace interruption. A 2007 study by Iqbal and Horvitz estimated that the average time to return to any suspended application after an e-mail interruption was 9 minutes, 33 seconds![3] These recovery estimates do not include the time it takes to respond to the actual message. Four minutes here to recover from an interruption, eight minutes there; one improperly forwarded e-mail here, one there; one poorly crafted memo here, one there...it all adds up to hours of wasted time each week.

E-mail productivity loss happens in very small chunks of time

In fact, Basex, an information-technology research firm in New York City, found that interruptions now consume an average of 2.1 hours a day, or 28 percent of the workday. The two hours of lost productivity included not only unimportant interruptions and distractions but also the recovery time associated with getting back on task, according to a Basex report titled "The Cost of Not Paying Attention," released in September. Estimating an average salary of $21 an hour for "knowledge workers"

---

3 Disruption and Recovery of Computing Tasks: Field Study, Analysis and Directions, S. Iqbal and Eric Horvitz, 2007

— those who perform tasks involving information — Basex calculated that workplace interruptions cost the U.S. economy $588 billion a year.[4]

Second, managers may not see the direct impact because many employees make up for the productivity shortfall on their own personal time. It appears that many loyal and committed employees continue to produce the results expected of them, even though their workday or workweek is lengthening because of communication overload. They work through lunch, arrive early, stay late, work from home, or work weekends to make up for the on-the-job productivity lost. One very committed employee recently lamented to me that, "because of all the e-mail I get, even thought I still have the same amount of work, I spend at least one more hour EVERY day at the office—and my boss has no idea that I do it!" This personal assumption of responsibility for the problem impedes the employer's ability to detect the productivity intrusion.

Workplace interruptions cost the U.S. economy $588 billion a year.

---

4 *Killer Pitch Blog 8/12/08; https://na5.brightidea.com/ct/ct_a_view_ idea.bi?order_flag=1&c=1636853C-E68B-4D48-AE3A- EE955F1BE352&peer_review=advanced&a= OD550&idea_id={6333B42C- F6DB-4F4B-8E40-C08209560627}*

When the loss of efficiency is masked by employee accommodation, the make-up time is taken from other areas of their lives, and may show up in the form of stress, lack of exercise, improper work-life balance, family problems, or other dysfunctional behavior. Employee well-being is unquestionably at risk when work demands unreasonably intrude into personal time. Although it may not directly affect the work produced, absence of work-life balance and increased stress will take its toll over time on employees and eventually on the morale and profitability of the business.

TOXIC SEDUCTION: AN EXAMPLE

Corporate culture is defined by the actions of the people who sit in the corner offices. Their habits, communication styles, and patterns of interactivity set the standard for the communication dynamics in the company they head. E-mail culture can be defined from the top down. If the C-level executives and the senior management team are online all the time, ambitious employees assume that one of the paths to success in this organization is rapid-fire response to e-mail anytime day or night. If the boss is using e-mail to communicate urgent information, the employee has no real choice but to check new messages as they come in for fear of missing a hastily-called meeting or a request for immediate action. If the CEO checks her PDA in the middle of meetings, permission to do the same is assumed. In the blink of an eye, compulsive e-mail behavior becomes a company-wide norm and soon the entire workforce is mirroring that behavior—becoming e-ddicted.

As I was being interviewed by a news reporter recently, she shared her exasperation and near disbelief about a situation experienced by one of her close co-workers. Her fellow employee, who last checked her e-mail at home just after 9:00 PM, arrived at work that day at 8:30 AM, her normal time, only to find that she missed an 8:00 AM meeting. In checking her e-mail, her boss had sent the meeting request just before midnight. This news shot around the office like wildfire.

In fact, if you are one of those employees attempting to practice savvy inbox management—for instance, by checking e-mail at only regularly scheduled intervals and keeping your inbox empty—you may be penalized for those practices which are out of sync with the company's e-mail culture.

Consider, for example, an urgent e-mail sent by the boss to three subordinates, summoning the employees to a can't-miss meeting to be held in fifteen minutes. Two of the three employees read the e-mail immediately and show up at the meeting. The third, busily working on a special project and trying to focus, has temporarily silenced his new message notification. He did not see the boss's e-mail and missed the meeting. When the boss expressed disappointment, the unstated lesson the employee learned is that he must immediately read every new e-mail received for fear of missing something important. He has just added a significant number of interruptions to his workday. He learned this lesson very quickly, and immediately integrates it into his practices. And it may not stop there. This manager may now start to use the same techniques with his subordinates.

What about the two employees who did see the e-mail right away and showed up at the meeting? Some executives and managers feel validated that e-mail can be used as an urgent delivery system—or should be, because their employees are accepting urgency as the new norm when it comes to e-mail. The employees now feel they have permission to make e-mail urgent. Very quickly, an entire workforce can shift from using e-mail as a useful delivery mechanism to using it as an urgent delivery system.

Defining the e-mail culture is the prerogative of the management team. Business leaders must understand the overall costs of either actively or passively endorsing compulsive or toxic e-mail behavior. All it takes is one phone call from the boss, who asks, "Didn't you read the e-mail I just sent you?" to send the not-so-subtle message that this business unit is expected to be always connected.

The good news is that it is possible to turn this waste of productivity around. By taking responsibility for the e-habilitation of the organization and using the techniques laid out in this book, optimal e-mail practices can be put into place that will increase the profitability the business, give the company an edge over the competition, and enable greater work-life balance for the workforce.

But just as poor e-mail habits can be infused from the top downward, so is the detox. To successfully conquer company-wide Inbox Detox and subsequently increase productivity, the transformation process starts at the top— the top of the company, the division, the work unit, or the cross-functional team can detoxify the entire group's e-culture. It is not only cultural, but it is individual.

When influential people change ingrained habits, they can truly impact the bottom line. When leaders spearhead the detoxification and set the standard for savvy e-mail practices among employees, everyone benefits. The overwhelmed employee no longer feels alone.

Without formal training, people have a tendency to learn "just enough" to get their work done. Instead of learning all the features of their e-mail programs, workers stop exploring the capability of the software when they have achieved a comfort level that enables them to perform their jobs. This is human nature — we've all done it. So, even though most commercial e-mail programs have efficiency tools built in, many are not used.

> **People have a tendency to learn "just enough" about e-mail to complete their tasks.**

Habits develop through the repetition of certain actions. With enough repetition, those habits become ingrained. Absent any direction, people create their own routines. As e-mail became an increasingly important part of daily communications, people applied their own time-management practices to e-mail use—some very efficient, but also some that have not served them well.

Ultimately, why are we concerned with e-mail habits? It comes down to numbers. When handling only a handful of messages, whether they are processed effectively or ineffectively, an employee is unlikely to experience a major infringement on his or her productive time. However, when that same employee receives hundreds of messages daily, the chances are strong that he or she continues to practice whatever habits were developed in the earlier, less hectic time. If those habits are unproductive, the wasted seconds turn into wasted minutes, which turn into wasted hours. Many e-mailers have passively fallen into poor inbox management and require focused re-education to break the inefficient habits.

> **Many e-mailers have passively fallen into poor inbox management.**

Take for example the employee who sends a copy of every e-mail to herself, just so that she will have a copy. (You may laugh, but a participant in one of my seminars admitted doing this!) Obviously, this person has never taken the time to learn about the "sent mail" feature of her program. This bad habit won't take much time out of her workday as long as her message volume is low, but if she sends 100 e-mails per day and copies herself on each, the time wasted becomes significant. It won't be difficult to identify the cure for this inefficient practice, but getting this person to shift to a more productive habit takes focus, and a trigger for her to recognize that there is a better way.

Behaviors are hard to change. The challenge is to help people break inefficient habits that they started when they were processing only a few e-mails a day, and to embrace new habits that will enable them to work more effectively. Easy concept, and yet difficult to truly change.

It starts with an acknowledgement or recognition of your productivity-sapping habits. How can you focus on a behavioral shift without an understanding of what needs to change?

The next chapter will help you identify those opportunities to reclaim that precious time you've been losing.

THE EVALUATION

This chapter starts with you; it contains a self-analysis tool that allows you to honestly assess your e-mail practices and determine whether or not they are toxic. After taking this assessment, you will have a greater understanding of your own e-mailing practices. You'll see what opportunities you have to increase your own productivity, thereby setting the stage for less stress, better organization, and greater impact.

INCOMING E-MAIL AND INBOX MANAGEMENT

Complete the following survey: *Rate yourself 1 to 5, with 5 meaning "Strongly Agree," and 1 meaning "Strongly Disagree", on this survey:*

I am not distracted when email arrives in my inbox.	
All bells, dings, flashes and notifications of newly received emails are turned off.	
My "automatic send/receive" is either turned off or set to at least 90 minutes.	
I check my email no more than 5 times during the workday.	

I open my email with the intention of sorting the new email rather than working it.	
My inbox is empty after handling/sorting my newly received email.	
I place emails in folders, and use folders to manage my work.	
I use rules to automatically handle received emails.	
I can easily find emails that require my action.	
I can find email messages over 2 weeks old within three minutes.	
I use diaries and reminders to manage my work.	
I set a time aside, daily, to plan my work for the day.	
I do a good job of sticking to my daily plan.	
I avoid letting my email pull me away from more important tasks.	
I regularly purge my email folders such as "Sent Mail."	
I close or minimize my email when I am working on other projects.	
I use the electronic calendar to schedule meetings and keep appointments.	
I use the phone, meetings or personal visits when communications can be complicated, confusing, or misinterpreted.	
I set boundaries around when I handle my email and when I turn it off.	
Email does not stress me out.	
TOTAL	

OUTGOING E-MAIL AND E-MESSAGE WRITING

Complete the following survey: *Rate yourself 1 to 5, with 5 meaning "Strongly Agree," and 1 meaning "Strongly Disagree", on this survey:*

I copy only the people who truly need to receive the information.	
I don't send BCCs.	
I make sure my group lists contain the correct audience for the message.	
I avoid using group e-mails as a way to share complicated opinions or to brainstorm.	
My e-mail messages are extremely brief and to the point.	
The main point, conclusion, or request is in the first sentence of my message.	
The subject lines of my e-mail messages are extremely detailed.	
For very short messages, I use the subject line as the message.	
I never send urgent e-mails.	
I never send e-mails when I am emotional or angry.	
I never use e-mails to provide "constructive criticism."	
I keep up with my e-mails regularly and avoid "dumping" a large amount of e-mail all at one time on my associates.	
I clean up forwarded e-mails so the reader can get to the point quickly.	
I use correct grammar, punctuation, and spelling in all my e-mails.	
I attach an autosignature that has all of my contact information to all e-mails.	
I attach attachments before hitting SEND.	
I use upper and lower case.	
I avoid abbreviations, emoticons, smiley faces, or "stationary."	
I craft messages with the reader in mind.	
I review the message thoroughly, and THINK before I hit SEND.	
TOTAL	

SCORES:

Handling Incoming E-mail: _____

Handling Outgoing E-mail: _____

For each assessment, consult the following scoring grid:

85-100: Congratulations — you are e-mail savvy! You have taken control of your e-mail.

70-84: You are well on your way to e-mail control — a few tweaks, and you're there. Scour the tips in this book to see where changes may be mandated. Also, take a look at the questions above to see where you may have some room for improvement.

50-69: Your e-mail attitudes and habits may be getting in your way. Time to make some changes! Begin by taking another look at the assessment survey you just took: on which questions did you rate unfavorably? Those questions represent your weak points, the areas on which you need to work for better e-habits. You will find great ideas for implementing e-mail best practices in Part II of this book.

35-49: Your e-mail habits need plenty of work. Take action to own your e-mail—now! Review the chapter on the 12 steps to managing your inbox and consciously work towards changing your e-mail habits.

21-34: Your e-mail habits are seriously hurting you and possibly those around you, whether you know it or not. Start now to change the way you manage your e-mail, and you'll find more hours in each day.

So, how did you do? Any score less than perfect outlines an opportunity for you to add more hours to your day— hours for what is truly important!

Just remember, the intent of these surveys is to highlight the opportunities that exist in your own e-mail handling. By taking an honest look at how you manage your e-mail, our hope is that your eyes will be opened to the possibilities that exist before you, first individually, then for your organization.

Each of these practices, and others, are explored in more detail throughout this book. Each shift will open the door to progress. Let's get started.

To take this assessment on line, please visit
http://InboxDetox.com/assessments

THE DIAGNOSIS

You've just taken two assessments. How did the numbers add up? If you've determined that there is room to grow, practices you can change, or opportunities to make room for the more important stuff in your life, then you've got the diagnosis. You have already taken a step by purchasing this book. You want something different. You want to change.

You must understand that if you are serious about taking control of your e-mail, you must first acknowledge where you can improve, so that your change efforts will be meaningful.

Which areas are affecting your productivity or effectiveness the most? Write them here:

_____

_____

_____

_____

_____

You've just acknowledged the areas that will benefit from some attention.

So, now you're in position to take the actions that will lower your stress and make room for what is really important in your life.

ADDICTION OR BAD HABIT?

For those of who have wondered whether you or others around you might have an addiction, we've provided some information below.

There has been a lot of attention given to whether people can be addicted to their e-mail. Whether it is an addiction or a bad habit, your recognition of the problem or opportunity opens the door for progress.

Addictive behavior occurs in two forms: substance addictions, which manifest when addictive substances like alcohol, caffeine, or drugs are ingested into the body, and process addictions. Process addictions occur as a result of a series of activities or interactions which cause a person to become dependent. Addictions in this category show themselves when people are hooked on gambling, work, sex, religion, and relationships. In its most extreme form, obsessive e-mail behavior can manifest as a process addiction. But there is a wide range of unhealthy practices that cause individuals to be unproductive and that, over time, can cause them to be continually distracted and lose control of their decision-making.

A recent news telecast featured a woman executive who "loved" her job, and "loved" her PDA even more. She proudly admitted that she checks her PDA constantly and just thrives on being in the thick of the corporate game. The segment showed her PDA next to the stove while she cooked dinner for her family, then showed her sneaking into the next room to check it as dinner was being served. Her husband and children, on national TV, declared that they wished she would be able to put it down during family time. In an independent interview, she swore that there was no problem.

Here are possible signs of an e-mail addiction. Addictive behavior can include:

- Choosing e-mail over career, relationship, family, or education
- Checking your e-mail incessantly
- Using e-mail as an escape
- Feeling restless and moody when detached from your e-mail
- Planning vacations to only places with Wi-Fi access
- Avoiding addressing concerns voiced by family and friends

Two people at a bar can be having the same drink, and one is an alcoholic and the other isn't. Same with e-mail; if you think you might have a problem, seek professional help in addition to applying the remedies in this book.

Like the heavy person who wants to lose 50 pounds and

keep it off, the solution is not rocket science. Deciding on the right diet and exercise routine is only the first step in losing that weight. It is the consistent healthy eating and disciplined exercise that will take the weight off and keep it off. We all know people who have lost weight only to gain it back...a classic symptom of temporarily changing without shifting habits.

The "cure" is not rocket science.

Whether it is an addiction or a bad habit, your misuse or mismanagement of e-mail impacts your personal and professional productivity. It is not healthy for you, your family, your co-workers, or your business.

Again, just like the weight loss analogy, detoxifying your e-mail habits doesn't offer the option of eliminating it. With some addictions, the treatment involves taking away the addictive substance. Unlike a harmful chemical that can gradually be eliminated, e-mail is ever-present in our work and personal lives. More like the person struggling with their weight, we must change the way we eat, rather than stop eating altogether. Likewise, e-mail is here to stay, and will most likely grow in velocity, so our best option is to manage it expertly and habitually.

> **Unlike a harmful chemical that can be eliminated, e-mail is ever-present in our work and personal lives.**

Then, there's the lighter side...here's a more humorous look at a possible "e-ddiction":

You know you're "e-ddicted" if...

- You e-mail yourself if you haven't received e-mail for several minutes, just to make sure the e-mail system hasn't gone down.
- You name your kids Mozilla, Firefox, and Google.
- You refer to yourself as your e-mail address when someone asks your name.
- You e-mail someone who has thanked you, thanking him or her for thanking you.
- You ask new acquaintances for their e-mail addresses, not their phone numbers.
- You sleep with your Blackberry nestled under your arm.
- You click "send/receive" incessantly just to make sure you haven't "missed" any e-mail.
- You e-mail the person sitting next to you, rather than turn around to ask the question.

Be it bad habit or addiction, let's begin the journey to conquering e-mail overload.

THE TIMELINE

Inbox detoxification requires an investment of time.

We believe that the underlying solution requires the taking on of new habits, not just acquiring new knowledge. Shifting habits requires consistent focus. It requires intentional repetition of the desired habit. It can't be done overnight. It takes time.

We recommend that you devote a minimum of one month of focus on these new processes, to learn and ingrain them. By the end of that time, your new habits will be second nature.

> ## Devote a minimum of one month to changing your e-habits.

The bad news is that you have to devote *at least* a month of focus to this effort.

The good news is that you have to devote *only* about a month of focus to this effort.

While shifting habits is not easy, it is not impossible either. It just requires focus.

So, are you willing to devote at least one month of focused attention to learning healthy e-mail habits?

Yes   No

THE DETOX PLAN

How many e-mails do you receive each day? If you are like the average business worker, you may receive anywhere from 80 to 150 e-mails daily. Without an effective way of dealing with this flood of e-mails, they can quickly overwhelm your inbox and invade your life.

Just like an addict going through detoxification, the first focus is "cleansing" your e-mail habits. That detox lies in first cleaning out your inbox, followed by the learning, application, and engraining of healthy practices. This book will guide you through the process.

> ## Start by cleansing your inbox.

To clean out your inbox, you'll learn the 12-Step Program: that's Part I. Once you've mastered that, you will use your new knowledge to empty that inbox. Then, in Part II, you'll learn over 100 tips that will reflect excellent, career-enhancing, eco-friendly, and respectful e-mailing practices that will help you maintain a perennially empty inbox.

We all know how great we feel those times when we have actually zeroed out our inboxes! Some people make a project of it over a weekend, some will shut their doors and "do e-mail" for hours until done, and some people secretly cheer when their system crashes and they lose all of those e-mails.

Having an empty inbox can feel like having an empty desktop: calm. There are no distractions. When our inboxes have nothing in them, we have nothing to pull us from that difficult project we need to start. Without those e-mails tugging at us, we are actually in a position to decide what we are going to do next—rather than go in there and try to knock off a few of those nagging e-mails collecting dust in your inbox. A clean inbox builds no stress. An empty inbox is key to inbox detoxification.

> **An empty inbox is the RESULT of your taking control of your e-mail and your life.**

And the reality is that if you're doing everything right, your inbox will be empty. An empty inbox is the RESULT of your taking control of your e-mail and your life.

OK, now you have your goal—an empty inbox. So the question is no longer "WHAT is the goal?" The question is "HOW do I get there?"

Here is the 12-Step Program that works.

THE 12 STEPS

Inbox Detox is not a one-time solution, nor is it a one-habit shift. It involves a series of steps that build upon each other. It involves replacing old habits with new ones, and it involves your willingness to make it all happen.

The 12 steps that follow are the steps that drew international acclaim in early 2007.

Even though your company may own your e-mail, the way you use your e-mail is essentially a private thing. It is rare that you find any employers looking over people's shoulders to determine whether their e-mail handling is the most efficient. Since the advent of electronic messaging, there has been little or no direction, much less instruction, on how to be most efficient with it. Similarly, no one is going to force you to rehabilitate your habits, even though you may recognize that they are getting in the way of your productivity and possibly your life.

> ## There has been little or no corporate direction on how to be most efficient with e-mail.

Embracing these 12 steps to has to come from within yourself. No one other than you can force a reformation of your habits. No one will be looking over your shoulder. You must want to take control of your e-mail and inbox under your own volition. And by learning, embracing, and committing to these 12 steps, you will form the framework to start repeating behaviors that you need to manage your inbox, and your life.

Inbox Detox is not achieved by merely emptying your inbox. Just like the person who loses 50 pounds without a change in eating behaviors, those 50 pounds will return in a few months. This 12-step approach focuses on how to MANAGE your e-mail, and more importantly, yourself. Self-management enables e-mail management, which lays the groundwork for your e-mail efficiency. It is the cornerstone upon which other success enabling habits can be built. Let's focus on how you can best manage your inbox.

> ## Self-management enables e-mail management.

So, are you ready to begin?

STEP 1: COMMIT TO CHANGE

Unless you are open and willing to trying and embracing new ways of doing things, you have wasted your money on this book. For you to detoxify that inbox, you will obviously have to do things differently. And most likely, you will need to change more than one habit or practice that you are currently following. Like an addiction, a dependency cannot be cured until it is acknowledged and faced head-on. You cannot overcome the limitations your bad e-mailing habits have on your professional effectiveness unless you admit that you have opportunities to improve or even that you've become a slave to your inbox. You've got to want to improve.

Admitting that you need to change may be difficult. Some people reading this book may even be addicted. Many people whose lives are being managed by e-mail believe that their behavior doesn't signify addiction, but rather simply constitutes a bad habit. Some people don't even view it as an obstacle. Regardless of the terminology, admitting the problem (and the opportunity) and wanting to change is a key ingredient to success. If you think there are opportunities for you to manage your time more effectively, then your admission is the first step toward serious progress.

> **Changing e-habits requires focus, perseverance, and a very conscious determination to do different things repeatedly.**

But that's only half the process: once you have acknowledged an opportunity, the next step is to make a personal commitment to alter your behavior. Changing habits requires focus, perseverance, and a very conscious determination to do different things repeatedly.

So, are you ready to change?

STEP 2: OWN YOUR E-MAIL

Do you own your e-mail or does it own you?

How many times has your telephone rung while you were having dinner with your family? Some people answer it, some don't. Some give the control of the moment to the ringing telephone, others take control and choose to let it ring, recognizing that the priority at that moment is the time spent with family. Which better describes you?

Just as some people feel compelled to answer the phone whenever it rings, others believe it is essential to respond to e-mails immediately upon receipt. Given the volume of e-mail you receive daily, perhaps it is difficult to tear your eyes away from the inbox, even when you're supposed to be working on other matters. This reactive approach is not only unnecessary, but it is a description of a classic inefficient practice.

You can operate under the same principle when it comes to your inbox. Don't allow yourself to be inconveniently sucked into time-wasting messages and exchanges that are not advancing a specific objective. Control the number of times you open your e-mail during your workday. Make overt decisions regarding your responses and manage the tasks that come your way just like you would with any other work assignment. Analyze your priorities and choose to be or not to be interrupted.

Become proactive rather than reactive. Own your e-mail, rather than allowing it to exercise power over you. That means you decide:

- when you will check for new messages and when you will respond
- when and how e-mail will fit into your daily plan
- when you will shut down your Blackberry or PDA
- what you will work on and when
- what sounds and reminders you will use or not use

Let go of a compulsion to respond to e-mails regardless of their importance. Let go of your assumptions that e-mails need to be responded to immediately. Let go of your checking your computer screen every 10 minutes for newfound treasure.

> # E-mail is a thing.
> # It doesn't think. You do.

By affirming, "I own my e-mail!" you have taken control. E-mail is a thing. It doesn't think. You do. When you take ownership of when and how you are going to manage your e-mail, you've opened the door for your successful control over your inbox.

So, have you decided to own your e-mail?

STEP 3: ESTABLISH REGULAR TIMES OR SPACED INTERVALS TO SORT YOUR E-MAIL

Owning your e-mail makes way for step three. Because you have committed to proactively manage and work your e-mail, you have enabled the freedom to choose when and how you will handle your e-mail and your inbox.

Taking control involves three steps that focus on minimizing your e-mail interruptions:

1. Turn off dings and reminders
2. Decide the maximum interval for checking e-mail
3. Establish a plan for retrieving e-mail

Why care about interruptions? Interruptions eat away at your time. E-mail interruptions can steal hours, not minutes. This Detox step alone could reclaim more time for you than all the others combined. Because time is money, it is prudent to reduce the number of daily e-mail interruptions to as few as possible.

According to the experts, each interruption the average person has takes an average of four minutes to recover— to "get back in the zone" after the interruption. E-mail is a huge interrupter for many people. By minimizing those e-mail interruptions, you will reclaim all of that time you lost recovering from each four-minute interruption.

Let's say you allow yourself to be interrupted by (only) 15 e-mails a day. Those 15 e-mails just cost you 60 minutes (15 x 4 minutes) recovering from those interruptions. If you shift to proactively checking your e-mail only FIVE times daily, (5 x 4 = 20 minutes) you just reclaimed 40 minutes in interruption recovery time—daily. Just think, if you receive 50 e-mails in one day, and have the reminders flashing and dinging every time one comes in, you could look up 50 times. That's 50 interruptions!

Here's how to eliminate or minimize those costly interruptions.

1. Close down your inbox or turn off all sound and visual reminders. Start by turning off any audio and visual signals that indicate a new message has arrived. Shutting off that "brrring" ensures that newly received e-mails will not become a routine distraction that continually interrupts the flow of your workday. Instead, you can initiate when you'll retrieve your e-mail. This places control in your hands.

2. Choose the appropriate intervals for checking e-mail. Second, decide the maximum interval that will work for you to either check your e-mail or to have the server deliver your e-mail. Focus on how infrequently you can retrieve your e-mail. Your business and customer needs will dictate what is best for you and your business. As you take ownership of your inbox, you will lengthen the amount of time between views of your inbox, you will minimize your interruptions and increase your ability to get high quality work done.

> ## Establish your plan for retrieving your e-mail.

3. Determine your plan for sorting e-mail. Third, establish your plan for retrieving your e-mail. Most employees in the average office setting can survive nicely with only checking their e-mail roughly five times daily:

- Upon arrival at work
- Mid-morning
- After lunch
- Mid-afternoon
- At the close of the business day

Better yet, consider checking your e-mail only twice daily! Just think how much more you and your associates can accomplish sorting e-mail only twice daily! For reasons we will discover later, the maximum interval you choose to view your inbox will help you achieve and maintain maximum productivity.

By having a plan and communicating it with others, you will manage their expectations and minimize your interruptions. You will also become more effective at organizing your day.

Turning off automatic receipt may not work for everybody, however. One alternative is to set your e-mail program to deliver your e-mails at set intervals. By setting up 60- or 90-minute intervals to receive new messages, you decrease your instantaneous automated interruptions to about seven times per workday.

Either of these options allows you to work systematically, checking e-mail only when it's convenient for you. Ultimately, you will increase your personal productivity by decreasing the amount of time e-mail handling eats up in your workday.

> ## There is a cost to continuous connectedness.

Your business and customer needs will dictate what is best for you and your business. Just recognize that there is a cost to continuous connectedness, and it is important that you and your company make a conscious decision about how often employees should be interrupted by e-mail.

Remember this: studies have shown that the majority of the e-mailers expect a return e-mail in roughly 24 hours, yet many recipients erroneously think they are expected to respond at lightning speed. Think about your own expectations—when you send an e-mail to someone else, do you expect an immediate response? When do you start wondering whether they received the e-mail? Most likely, your answer will not be immediate. Who knows? They may be in a meeting, they may be out of the office, they may be working on another project, they may be home with the flu. Why, then, do many e-mailers think that an immediate response is required?

> ## The majority of the e-mailers expect a return e-mail in roughly 24 hours.

We can apply this phenomenon to our taking control and spacing the intervals when we view our inboxes. We are not suggesting a nonresponse; we are advocating that a response within two to three hours in the strong majority of situations is quite acceptable.

At this point, many people going through the 12-Step Program ask this question: HOW can I maintain excellent customer service if I check my e-mail only 5 times a day?

Here's the answer: By grouping your tasks and minimizing your interruptions you will get more done, have higher quality work, AND respond in a reasonable time.

Again, we are not advocating not responding. We are challenging you to group the handling of your e-mail messages so that you will minimize your interruptions. We've already established that most e-mailers do not expect an immediate response. They expect a response in about 24 hours. So, if you view your e-mail five times in a day, the longest stretch you'll go is about two hours. If it is important, you can choose to respond at that time.

Your business and customer needs will dictate what is best for you and your business. There are some businesses that must have the ability of immediate response, such as the breaking news business. Just remember, there is a cost to continuous connectedness, and it's important that your company or work group makes a conscious decision about how often employees should be interrupted by e-mail.

We also get this question: What if my boss e-mails me and wants an immediate response?

Unfortunately, this is a symptom of a toxic e-mail behavior, and perhaps even a toxic e-mail culture ...

If and when your boss does this, he or she is promoting an urgent e-mail culture...and unfortunately urgent e-mail cultures are toxic cultures. They are toxic because they force all the employees to keep their e-mail open, dinging, and continually interrupting them. The cost to the organization is enormous just in interruption recovery time, and many bosses are oblivious to it.

One solution is to have a meeting with the urgent e-mailer or the workgroup impacted to develop an agreement that anything needed in less than three hours will be handled in person or by telephone. More on urgent e-mails later ... it is important that you commit to minimizing your e-mail interruptions.

So,

1. When will you turn off all visual and audio reminders?

2. What is the longest interval you'll use to check e-mail? How many times daily will you view your inbox?

3. When will you view your inbox?

STEP 4: CHANGE YOUR VIEW OF THE INBOX

Take a minute to think about your postal mailbox. As you pull your mail out, you might flip through each item deciding what you need to read, keep, and file—and what you can just toss out. What you probably don't do, however, is look through the envelopes, magazines, and postcards you received and then stick them back in your mailbox!

> # Your inbox is not a holding tank—it is a delivery tool.

Likewise, the inbox is not a holding tank—it is a delivery tool. Just as your postal mail isn't meant to stay piled up in your postal mailbox, your e-mail messages aren't meant to reside in your inbox. They need to be moved or handled.

By embracing the understanding that your inbox is not a "to do" list or the place where you keep messages to remind you to perform the tasks requested in the message, you open the door for much greater efficiency in handling all of the work delivered to you by e-mail.

Getting back to the mailbox example, you most likely also sort that mail after you've taken it into your home ... trash, handle immediately, save for later, read. Not unlike the actions required of messages received in your inbox.

Too many people confuse sorting e-mails and handling e-mails as one task. They are not. To be most effective at managing your inbox, it is important to understand and embrace the distinction between the two. The inbox delivers. You sort. Sorting denotes viewing, grouping, moving, and assessing priorities, while handling means actually working within the details of the e-mail. You need to commit to sort the work delivered by e-mail, and then

53

handle it in the priority that it deserves. Each time you go into your inbox, it should be with the intention to sort your mail, not handle it, just as you manage your postal mail.

We'll show you how to handle messages in your inbox in later steps.

> **Too many people confuse sorting e-mails and handling e-mails as one task.**

We liken this process to that of an emergency room nurse. The nurse "triages" patients based on their priority, not based on when they arrived or how quickly they can be served. Instead, patients are triaged according to priority. As an example, a person with a head injury will be seen immediately, while someone with a broken finger may wait for hours. This is the way we need to approach our incoming e-mail in order to reach a state of Inbox Detox.

E-mail itself is not a task. It delivers tasks. When you shift your thinking from, "I've got to do e-mail," to "I've got work to do" (regardless of whether it was delivered by e-mail or a visit by the boss,) you are on the road to better and faster results. This shift can happen when you change your view of the inbox.

So, do you now see your inbox as a message delivery tool?

STEP 5: EMPTY YOUR INBOX EVERY TIME YOU VIEW IT

This is the step that gives people the shakes. But—to truly and perennially detoxify your inbox—it is critical that you learn, practice, and embrace it.

Leaving e-mail messages you have already read in your inbox is just as counter-productive as leaving old mail in the box at the end of your driveway. Yet people routinely leave received items in their inboxes, even after they have been read. This transforms the inbox into one enormous pending file. "Even though we're spending more time managing the same e-mail volume, our inboxes and mail files are growing in size," one recent survey concluded.[5] "Last year 51% said they keep 50 e-mails or less in the Inbox; this year that number is 39% while the percentage of people keeping 1000 or more messages in the Inbox almost doubled to 10%."

Over time, as e-mails pile up, the inbox becomes overloaded with tens, if not hundreds, of items to which you have not properly responded. As the number of new messages increases, employees experience unnecessary stress as the overflowing inbox reminds them of all the

---

5 *2006 E-mail Usage Survey," ClearContext Corporation, San Francisco, CA, May 2006.*

unfinished business that needs to be tended to. Scrolling up and down an overstuffed, disorganized inbox—looking for work assignments, or trying to locate a lost message—is an enormously futile, time-wasting activity. Keeping hundreds of items in your inbox is akin to having hundreds of uncategorized unfinished papers on your desk—distracting, disorganized, and stressful.

Thanks to our traditional view of inboxes, this concept is perhaps the most difficult to grasp in the detox program. Bad habits may have trained you to expect to see old or recently viewed messages in our inboxes. However, you should only see new, unread messages when you open your inbox folder. As this new mail is delivered, you should sort it, handle it, or trash it—but never keep it in the inbox.

This practice works in concert with Step 3; when you retrieve your e-mail at widely spaced intervals throughout the day you allow grouping enough e-mails for a productive sort. Remember, emptying your inbox does not mean handling every item immediately; it means sorting, deleting, responding, and moving items to the appropriate places that allow you to better manage your work. We will show you where to move them in Step 6.

The main goal of proper inbox maintenance is to keep your inbox available for newly-received items.

> **Emptying your inbox does not mean handling every item immediately; it means sorting them.**

By flushing your inbox each time you open it, you will be able to clearly label items, find them more easily, and respond appropriately to messages when the time is right. This way, you also avoid a serious accumulation of messages that need a response but ultimately get lost in the shuffle. After all, nobody wants to have to send a message that reads, "I'm so sorry it has taken me so long to respond to you; I have just been going through old e-mails and realized I'd never responded to your message." By keeping your inbox clean and manageable, you will have a failsafe system in place to ensure that every message receives a response.

So, are you committed to emptying your inbox, every time you view it?

STEP 6: CREATE E-FOLDERS

Keeping numerous e-mails in your inbox is akin to keeping all of your paper tasks strewn all over your desk. There is no organization, no priority, no categorization. Your efforts to keep your inbox empty will hinge on the effectiveness of the e-mail folder system you establish to manage your messages. In order to implement best e-mail practices and to take control of your inbox, here are some simple organizational steps that will help you manage the e-mails you receive.

Similar to any other business task, e-mail management greatly benefits from having some organization. Specifically named e-mail folders allow messages to maintain importance without clogging up the inbox. By creating separate folders to store e-mails that have arrived in your inbox, you are taking a proactive approach to the problem rather than a reactive method that will lead to stress down the line.

Although no two persons' e-mail folders will be the same, most effective e-mail filing systems will share some basic components. Their contents, organization, and specifics will vary by person and industry.

Just remember — electronic folders are your key to the ultimate Inbox Detox.

What should your e-mail filing system look like? We have refined a simple way to organize e-folders that works...

58

You will need two basic categories of folders: action folders and reference folders. Action folders contain anything that requires action by you. Reference folders are for all other items that do not require action, but contain information that you may need at a future time.

Action folders are where you hold items requiring action. They do not replace your diary system, they are simply where the messages requiring your action reside. In other words, whatever system you're using to keep track of your work and remind you when to work on tasks needs to remain intact—you'll use that system to remind you to access the work being held in your Action Folders.

Unfortunately, most people merge action and reference folders, contributing to confusion and inability to find critical work. Your ability to keep these concepts separate will help you get more done and in the right priority.

Action Folders

Action Folders are the backbone of your e-mail work management system.

They are the folders that hold any items that require your action. Having them in a central place will enable easy access and workload prioritization. Each person's action folders will be different, so spend some time looking at your e-mail, specifically. Your influx of e-mail will dictate what action folders you need.

Place messages requiring your action into ACTION Folders.

It is important to note that these action folders DO NOT replace your diary system. For each message requiring action, you should create a diary to retrieve it. Whether you use a paper diary system, or an electronic one, use the diary system that works best for you. Your diary will trigger your finding the message easily in your Action Folders.

Action folders do NOT replace your diary system.

People spend way too much time searching for e-mail messages containing task assignments, either within their inboxes, or among a wide variety of folders. This folder system simplifies it.

Place e-mail messages in an Action Folder if they require you to do something with it. For each important item, set a flag, a diary, or task to remind you when to work on it. The more important the task, the more critical the diary. So as you sort your messages, the majority of those you drag and drop into an Action Folder will also require you to set a diary or reminder.

Here is how to set up your Action folders:

· Action – A

Here is where you place the items that have a high priority.

· Action – B

Here is where you place the items that have a lower priority, but still require your action.

Note: By starting the name of each Action Folder with the word, "Action," they will be grouped together alphabetically in your folder list. This makes the sort, drag, and drop even easier.

· Action – Pending

This folder should contain e-mails that are not complete, but for which you've done as much as you can do. Essentially, the Action – Pending Folder contains items that require action by someone else. It contains items that are not ready to be put in a reference folder — yet. So, if you have responded and are awaiting a response, place the e-mail to which you already responded in your Action – Pending Folder.

The above three folders are the backbone of an e-filing system that will enable you to achieve Inbox Detox and find the tasks you need to accomplish.

Sometimes, people will create an optional action folder that groups similar and frequent tasks—it is almost like having a pre- sort. Examples might be folders for industry reading or bill paying. Here is an example:

· **Action – Reading (optional)**

The Action – Reading Folder is an example of an optional Action Folder that has been created to group similar tasks. It houses e-mails that require you to read something, whether it's a trade newsletter or a notice of new procedures. When you are sorting your newly received e-mail, and you receive something that you would like to read—a classic important but not urgent task -- you can drag and drop it into the Action — Reading folder.

Just remember, the more folders you have, the more complicated your e-mail management. Quite frankly, e-mail folders with very broad subject headings work very well because of the technological ability to sort the messages by subject, sender, etc., unlike paper file system counterparts. It is always better to search within folders than among them. Therefore, we recommend no more than five action folders.

> ## It is always better to search within folders than among them.

Reference Folders

Reference Folders contain e-mails that don't need your attention. This is where you can save messages that you may want to refer to at a later date. While these e-mails hold no immediate relevance, you may need to refer back to them at another time. Examples include records of correspondence, procedures, quotes, contracts, and directions.

For all of your reference folders, opt for broad topics over narrow ones. The broader, the better. For example, use one e-mail file to store messages related to your benefits, rather than setting up several smaller folders for specific types of benefits. Broad folder headings will enable you to find the message you need more quickly, without having to guess which of several narrow folders might include the e-mail you're seeking.

Most e-mail programs allow you to change the subject of a received e-mail message. This feature can be used to help you enhance message subject lines for more efficient retrieval at a later date.

To be completely efficient in your office filing, you may consider synchronizing your e-mail Reference Folders with your paper files and hard drive folders. For example, if you have both a paper file and a hard drive folder for your benefits information, consider setting up the same e-mail file name, "Benefits," to store your benefits-related e-mails.

STEP 7: APPLY THE E-MAIL TWO-MINUTE RULE

Here's the golden rule of e-mail triage: The E-Mail Two Minute Rule.

If an e-mail can be handled and responded to in two minutes or less, then take care of it immediately. If not, the second you determine it will take you more than two minutes, stop reading and don't do any more with the e-mail—instead, set a diary to address it later, and file the e-mail in an appropriate action folder so that you can find it easily.

> **If an e-mail can be handled and responded to in two minutes or less, take care of it immediately.**

Mastering the Two-Minute Rule will allow you to clear out your inbox every time you go into it. It sustains e-mail efficiency. Let's say you've opened your inbox and you've received seven newly arrived e-mails. By adhering to this rule, you know that the most time you'll spend sorting and handling those e-mails is 14 minutes. And most likely, it will be much less, because you'll decide to file, trash, or handle most items in a few seconds.

The E-mail Two-Minute Rule needs to be applied regardless of the priority of the task, even if it is an extremely low priority. While this direction flies in the face of traditional time management wisdom, we believe it is necessary due to the sheer number of e-mails most of us receive daily. Getting rid of the quickly handled clutter trumps the priority of it.

> ## Getting rid of the quickly handled clutter trumps the priority of it.

Then, view each e-mail, in order, from top to bottom, or bottom to top. Resist the temptation to pick and choose the next e-mail you will view. Why? Because picking and choosing wastes time. Using the Two-Minute Rule, start at the top and handle the item until it is out of your inbox. Then go to the next. Then go to the next ... after you are finished, your inbox is again empty. See how this works?

One of the most damaging and unproductive e-mail management blunders is to become distracted by a low priority message. You assume that responding to the message won't take long, only to find yourself still working on it 20 minutes later. The E-mail Two-Minute Rule addresses this common trap.

Now that you've spent some time establishing and

organizing your e-mail filing system and learning the Two-Minute Rule, it's essential that you apply valuable time management skills that will help you effectively tackle those e-mails you've placed into your e-mail folders.

So, will you apply the Two-Minute Rule every time you sort your e-mail?

STEP 8: SET A REGULAR TIME TO PLAN YOUR DAY

One of these most frequent objections or fears we hear with this system of triaging and using folders is the concern that once an item is filed, it will be forgotten. This can be a legitimate concern if you don't have a system that prevents it.

Here is the answer:

Establish a consistent time each day to plan your work. Some people prefer first thing in the morning, others find it makes more sense to schedule at the end of the day. This is the time when you plan ALL of your daily activities, including phone calls, projects, meetings, and tasks delivered by e-mail. Open your diaries to decide which of those tasks you will choose to work on during the day. Then find them easily in the appropriate action folders.

> **Establish a consistent time each day to plan your work.**

Toxic e-mail habits have diffused the importance of daily planning, a key component of time management. People allow the delivery of new messages to continually interrupt and impose on their daily plan. Prioritizing your tasks each day gives you a daily roadmap that will help you resist the tempting interruptions brought by new e-mail.

Let's assume that you'll take the first half-hour of your morning to plan your schedule for the day and to decide which tasks need your attention. In the planning process, you need to assess e-mail delivered tasks the same way you prioritize other work-related tasks such as return phone calls, meetings, and projects. Once daily, gather and assess ALL your work priorities, and make decisions about how and when you can best use your time. This is when you plan meetings, prioritize tasks and phone calls, access your diary system, find the appropriate messages in your action folders, and set the appropriate schedule that will enable great results for the day.

As we said earlier, one of the biggest fears for people in the 12-Step Inbox Detox Program is that they will file messages in an action folder and forget them. Making it a habit to properly plan and prioritize your day ensures that you won't forget about the diaried tasks in your action folders.

While this Inbox Detox program is not intended to be a time management primer, the basic time-management concept of once-a-day planning is key to making sure e-mail delivered tasks are handled efficiently and in the right priority.

A classic e-mail handling blunder is to allow newly received unimportant e-mail messages to detour your daily plan.

Most successful businesspeople have one thing in common: They have a plan and they work that plan. Productive e-mail users are no different. They take time to organize their days, and stick to that plan, allowing for reasonable (but not continuous low priority e-mail) interruptions.

So, when will you schedule your daily planning time?

STEP 9: BUDGET TIME TO SORT E-MAIL

Plan to sort your e-mail messages.

Too many people underestimate the amount of time sorting their e-mail will consume. However, e-mail is becoming an increasingly significant part of most people's work that requires systematic and continuous attention. Sorting e-mail-delivered tasks must be included in the daily schedule that is planned in Step 8.

Determine the amount of time you'll need to spend sorting e-mails each day, and set aside that time on your schedule or to-do list like any other business task. By building time into your schedule, inbox management becomes an expectation in your daily routine rather than an annoyance that catches you off guard at inconvenient times.

Take the average number of e-mails you receive per day, divide by the number of times you'll check your inbox, and multiply by two minutes—that's the maximum amount of time it should take you each time you check your inbox. And remember, many of the e-mails you receive will take only seconds to process, either by the leading or filing into e-folders, so two minutes per item is the absolute maximum amount of time.

Schedule times to sort your e-mail.

The times of day and amount of time you'll need to spend sorting your e-mail will depend on your specific schedule and work demands—and your discipline. Note that this strategy means not checking e-mail every five minutes, or even every hour; it means no automatic reception of incoming and outgoing mail; it means no peeking into your inbox "just in case something important has come in."

By setting up specific and well-spaced times to sort your e-mail as described in Step 3, and budgeting time to sort the newly received e-mail, you'll eliminate interruptions, stop wasting precious time, keep pace with your e-mail volume, and be more productive.

So, how much time and when will you plan to sort your e-mail messages?

STEP 10: REDUCE THE AMOUNT
OF E-MAIL YOU RECEIVE

E-mail begets e-mail. By reducing the number of e-mails you send daily, and by implementing some simple steps when sending e-mail, you will in return reduce the number of e-mails you receive.

There is no question that people who use e-mail more frequently than others receive more e-mails in response.

Ask yourself, "Is this e-mail really necessary?" Consider that each e-mail you send to one recipient could create at least one return e-mail. For messages sent to groups, there can be a multiplier effect. By envisioning every e-mail you send as a potential trigger for a return e-mail, you will help yourself receive less e-mail.

E-mail begets e-mail.

Below are some other ways to minimize the e-mail coming into your inbox. More detailed techniques of each are explored further in Part II of this book: E-mail Excellence. Here is a quick summary of e-mail reducing practices:

Pick up the phone. Situations requiring true dialogue are best served with a phone call. Many times even a voice mail message can be better in advancing the conversation.

Avoid emotion. Argumentative, emotional, or controversial e-mails should not be sent; they not only create more angst, but generally create more e-mail response.

Use an autosignature. Be sure your e-mail signature line contains all of your contact information. A detailed signature line will make it easy for others to call you or contact you instead of e-mailing, thereby saving the overall transaction time.

Resist temptation. Don't fall into the trap of responding to e-mails just because you feel you need to—if an e-mail truly doesn't require your reply, let it go and save valuable time.

Clear, concise, short e-mails. Well-crafted and clear e-mails avoid misunderstandings and return e-mails to you asking for clarification.

Main point first. Place your main point, assignment, or request within the first two lines of an e-mail can get your reader focused on exactly what you want right from the get-go.

Copy the right recipients. If you copy people extraneously, you are not only generating more messages for them, but also risking receiving an unnecessary response yourself.

Proofread your e-mail. By making sure that the content of your message is understandable, you will avoid a barrage of reply questions in your inbox.

So, what actions will you take to reduce the amount of e-mail you receive?

STEP 11: INVOLVE OTHERS

One of the best ways to ensure that you stay on track and won't "fall off the wagon" is to involve others in your plans to change your e-mail habits and practices. Particularly at your workplace, you can gain much support by simply including your coworkers and employees in your plan to turn your e-mail habits and practices around.

Detail your Inbox Detox plans to your colleagues and employees. Let people know that you've turned off automatic send and receive, and that you've changed your e-mail viewing habits to five times a day or to 60- to 90-minute intervals — so, should they need to contact you urgently, they should call or stop by instead of e-mailing. Also, practice what you preach by avoiding creating unnecessary e-mails and work for others, and simply pick up the phone more often.

> **Involve others in your plans to change your e-mail habits.**

Finally, don't be afraid to ask for help. You may be surprised at people's reactions, and may even find that you're setting a positive example for coworkers and employees, encouraging them to implement e-mail best practices as well.

72

So, who will you involve in your Inbox Detox Program?

STEP 12: CELEBRATE SUCCESS

Now that you know the Inbox Detox 12-Step Program, you can understand how your inbox no longer needs to control you. You are free to maximize your productivity in your professional and personal life.

Taking control of your inbox is cause celebrate.

It sets you up to build on even more efficiencies in how you handle your e-mail. Think back at how the process worked for you, and what the most important thing was that you learned through its implementation. Then, take a moment to celebrate and promise yourself that you'll stay committed to having a perennially empty inbox. Every day. Every time you open your e-mail.

> # Celebrate your achievement!

Celebrating success is an important step. It confirms and solidifies your commitment to taking control of your inbox and your life. Don't skip this step. Decide how you will celebrate, then celebrate your achievement.

So, how will you celebrate your conquering the Inbox Detox 12-Step Program?

THE CLEANSING

We're not done. Knowing the methods to keeping your inbox under control is a great start. These 12 steps pave the way for complete efficiency and productivity with this new technological tool. It paves the way to your future success. But first, we have one big cleansing to do.

If you are like many of my clients, you didn't buy Inbox Detox because your inbox was empty... Most likely, you have many items in that inbox.

So before you can get into a daily regimen that honors the 12 steps, you need to cleanse that inbox, once and for all.

The next action then, is to plan to get your current inbox down to zero. This Inbox Detox program won't work well without you taking this very important step.

Don't groan. Having many items in your inbox is actually an advantage—it will create a focused effort on emptying that inbox that will help you actually ingrain the habits that will maintain inbox control in the future!

And here is the method that will work.

Set a date. The best way to get this done is to set a target date.

Here is some help in setting up your target date. Using the two-minute rule as your guide, take the number of e-mails you currently have in your inbox and multiply them by two minutes. This is the maximum amount of time you'll need to budget. We believe you're safe cutting that time in half, then half again, because many of the e-mail messages will take only seconds to handle. Divide that number by 60 minutes, and you will have an estimate of how many hours it will take you to empty that inbox. We suggest that you break this effort into no more than one-hour segments.

So, using the formula above, if you have 250 e-mails, the most time it should take you to empty your inbox will be 500 minutes, or eight hours. The reality is many of those items won't take you two minutes, but eight hours would be the maximum amount of time. Our better guess would be that it might take you two to four hours...so you might want to plan an hour a day for the next three or four days as your target.

Realizing that this cleansing is an investment in your professional and psychological future, give yourself some space, and don't try to do it all at once or it will drive you crazy.

Some people have devoted an hour a day, every other day until they achieved their zero goal. Others devoted a half hour every morning. Still others set aside time daily on consecutive days. Do what works best for you, but don't stop until you get to zero.

Caution! Practice the right habits. As you do your Inbox Detox sweep, it is important that you use the e-mail two-minute rule, file things in folders, and set diaries as you would after you have reached the zero items in your inbox. Apply the steps you learned in the 12-Step Program.

As my niece, Alison, once corrected me when I admired her piano practice, saying, "Practice makes perfect" she stated, "No, Auntie Moo, Perfect practice makes perfect." Avoid being romanced into handling any item that will take you more than two minutes. Avoid unnecessary scrolling. Avoid working on low priority stuff. If you don't, you will ingrain toxic habits rather than change them.

Some people have had success creating a temporary review folder, and moving everything from the inbox to that folder. They achieved an empty inbox immediately. This method can work, only if you commit to going into that temporary review folder, and sorting the e-mail messages contained therein by your target date.

There is a silver lining in this ... emptying that e-mail inbox is actually a great exercise in affirming the new habits you will develop for handling your e-mail. Because it is a concentrated effort, you will learn what you repeat, thereby shortening the amount of time to ingrain new habits.

Set a target date, right now, by which your inbox will be totally empty. Make the target date realistic, and commit to it.

So, when will your inbox be completely empty? _____

PART II

NEW HABITS

THE EXCELLENCE HABIT

You've already read and begun to implement the personal and organizational inbox management best practices detailed by the 12 steps. They form the foundation for managing yourself and your inbox. But best practices go even farther than that.

Each e-mail sent or reviewed offers an opportunity to add to or steal from your daily allotment of time, as well as from your own personal productivity.

> **Each e-mail you send or receive can steal time from you.**

On the surface, some of these suggestions may seem inconsequential. Just remember that each practice, even if it drains a mere three seconds of productivity, can significantly impact your life if done repeatedly. Those reclaimed seconds add up—to e-mail excellence.

Try each one of these. Make them habits. And add hours to your days.

PICK UP THE PHONE

One of the most effective ways to manage your e-mail, ironically, is to pick up the phone more often. Avoid sending an e-mail in situations where it makes more sense to give a call. Many times, a simple phone call avoids a barrage of unnecessary e-mails. For example, if the issue requires in-depth discussion, or may incite arguments or disagreements, you are better off calling instead of typing out lengthy back and forth responses.

Even if you connect via voice mail, you'll have the advantage of voice inflection and more words of explanation that can advance the conversation.

Some people can't resist calling you 10 minutes after they send you an e-mail to "make sure you received it." In addition to fostering a toxic urgent e-mail culture and causing an additional interruption, this practice is just plain annoying!

If you have an issue that requires immediate attention, call first to notify the recipient that he or she should view his or her e-mail, not the other way around.

> **Toxic E-mailer Alert**
>
> ## DOUBLE-CHECKING DILLY
>
> *Dilly sends an e-mail, and then calls you a few minutes later to see if you received it.*
>
> **Dilly's Antidote:** *If it is that important, and she wants to make sure the recipient gives her e-mail the attention she believes it deserves, Dilly should call first to advise that the e-mail is forthcoming, and to explain the reason for its priority.*

AVOID URGENT E-MAILS

For anything that is urgent, make the phone call. If you need a response in less than three hours, make the phone call. Avoid using e-mail urgently, and foster this practice among your co-workers—you'll be amazed at how much additional time your workgroup, collectively, will regain.

Urgent e-mails are toxic. Once your culture has "adopted" the use of urgent e-mails, people feel compelled to keep their inboxes open, dinging and flashing. In other words, it fosters a culture of interruption.

> **Urgent e-mails are toxic.**

We've all met this boss—the one who uses e-mail to call urgent meetings to request a teleconference within the next five minutes, or to ask employees to bring something important to a meeting beginning in a few minutes.

Does this look familiar? (Bold emphasis added)

From: Ursula
To: Greg, Anita, Debbie, Maddie
Sent: Wednesday, September 22, **9:47 AM**
Subject: Sales Report

Please bring this sales report to today's **10:00** staff meeting. Thanks. Ursula

Toxic E-mailer Alert

URGENT URSULA

Urgent Ursula sends e-mails when she needs something ASAP. She expects that her subordinates have their e-mail open and are anxiously awaiting her electronic gifts. She doesn't consider that her employees could be trying to manage their daily plans. Sometimes Ursula almost enjoys the power that it represents.

Ursula's Antidote: *Ursula should never send urgent e-mails. E-mail was not established to be an urgent communication tool. If she ever has anything urgent or needed in less than three hours she should call or visit. If this is happening too much, she should take a good look at herself and figure out why so many things on her plate are urgent.*

RESIST TEMPTATION: YOU DON'T NEED TO RESPOND TO EVERY E-MAIL

Don't fall into the trap of responding to e-mails just because you feel you need to—if an e-mail truly doesn't require your reply, let it go and save valuable time—for you and the recipient. For instance, resist getting involved in threads that don't concern your work—the sender may have copied you erroneously or extraneously. Consider the e-mail's relative importance to your position and work, because once you respond, you have "put yourself into the game."

> **Every e-mail you send should add value or advance the conversation.**

Though often meant as a courtesy, several of my clients say that one of the more frustrating e-mails they receive is the e-mail that merely responds with the word, "thanks." Like similar one-word wonders, such as "great," or "OK," this practice is another time-waster for the recipient who must open and read the e-mail—not to mention recover from the annoyance of having had to deal with it. Remember, every time someone opens an e-mail, a few more seconds are stolen from something more important.

> **Toxic E-mailer Alert**
>
> ## THANKFUL THELMA
>
> *Thelma responds to just about every e-mail, even if it is to merely say "thank you."*
>
> **Thelma's Antidote:** *Thelma doesn't need to respond to every e-mail. She should be judicious in her return "thanks." Every e-mail she sends should add value or advance the conversation.*

ONE SUBJECT PER E-MAIL

To avoid confusion, individual subjects, topics, or ideas should have their own e-mail messages. Too many times, people combine more than one subject in an e-mail to multiple recipients. Remember that most readers skim. Combining subjects increases the possibility that the second or third subject is missed. In many cases, not all recipients are interested in both messages, creating confusion, double filing, and unnecessary reading—all time wasters, if not for you, for them. To avoid confusion and to minimize the chance that the second message will be missed, consider creating a separate e-mail with a separate subject line for each topic.

This practice is most effective when you're tempted to include two or three things that aren't related or equally important all recipients. Be guided by being considerate of each recipient's time.

In the example below, there are least two subjects or requests for Jon, Susan, and Pat, and the second part is just for Pat. Jon and Susan will waste time reading something unrelated to them.

> Hi Jon, Susan, and Pat,
> Attached is my recommendation on our marketing campaign. I will present it at our next staff meeting, and will appreciate your feedback and ideas before the meeting.
>
> Pat, I have an old college friend that I heard is working for SVC now. His name is Matt Kennedy. Would you mind getting in touch with him on your next SVC visit?
> Jody

The inefficiencies caused by multi-subject e-mails can become compounded as the number of recipients increase. Because people have a tendency to "reply to all," everyone copied is compelled to read all subjects, even though one or more of these specific requests have nothing to do with them. In the above example, if Pat hits "reply all" in his response about Matt Kennedy, Jon and Susan will have another unnecessary e-mail to handle.

ASSUME YOUR READERS SKIM

Whether you read every single word of every e-mail you receive or not, a recent study showed that most people read only about 50 percent of an e-mail message.[6] So, when crafting your message, take extra caution to make sure your request is very clear, very easily found, and direct. The shorter the e-mail, the more likely all of its content will be read.

> # The shorter the e-mail, the more likely all of its content will be read.

Using this example, ask yourself how quickly you are able to determine the main point or request of the first paragraph.

> Hi John,
>
> As you know, the reorganization of our polymerization process is one of the most important projects we will undertake this physical year. Of course, the feasibility of the whole project depends on the fact that production costs would diminish over time, which your calculations showed would have been. The Executive Committee would like to see the analysis on which this projection was based. Could you please send me the original engineering documents?
>
> We have already made substantial progress in implementing the plan. The Executive Committee was

---

6 Jeanniey Mullen, ClickZ 2005   www.clickz.com

> going to discuss this at their June meeting, but the meeting got pushed up to May. They reviewed the design with minimal changes, so that puts us ahead of schedule. If you and Susan could take a look at their comments and respond to them, that would be very helpful. Then I can get the documents back to them in time for their next meeting. Thanks!
> Larry

If you had to read and reread the paragraph, just think about how much extra time other recipients might waste.

A more effective message could look like this:

> Hi John,
>
> Please send me the original engineering documents for the polymerization project by Tuesday.
>
> The Executive Committee has requested the analysis on which this projection was based, especially your calculations showing that production costs would diminish over time.
>
> Thanks, Larry

WRITE THE MAIN POINT, ASSIGNMENT, OR REQUEST IN THE FIRST TWO SENTENCES

In addition to modeling a well-written letter or memo, writing the main point in the first line of the e-mail message reduces the potential for an item to be missed or misinterpreted. As you can see in the second example above, your reader should be able to easily determine the main point or request.

Toxic E-mailer Alert

BURIER BOB

Bob buries the main point of his e-mails in the middle of the message, using his stream of thinking as the track for the correspondence. The result? Few people can find the point, let alone understand it and respond to it quickly!

Bob's Antidote: It will be much more effective for Bob to include his main point or request within the first two lines of an e-mail—that way, his ideas come across strong and his recipients are spared a trip through Bob's cranium in search of it. Remembering that the majority of readers skim, placing the primary point or request in the first sentence minimizes potential reading errors. Bob will benefit because it will most likely take the reader less time to read and understand.

WRITE BRIEF, CLEAR, AND CONCISE MESSAGES

While this helpful hint may appear to be a "no brainer," it may be one of the most important e-mailing strategies you can have. We already know that most readers skim. The longer the message the more words there are to skim, and the more potential for content to be missed or misinterpreted. By making sure that the content of your message is understandable, you will also avoid a barrage of reply questions in your inbox.

The shorter the e-mail message, the better.

A classic e-mail time management error is to spend a great deal of time composing a very detailed and complex e-mail on a subject that would be much more appropriately discussed. It takes much more time to type than to talk. Are people hiding behind e-mail? Are they trying to avoid discussion? Are they lazy? The more efficient tactic is to discuss the issue or recommendation in person or by phone, then confirm the major points by e-mail.

> ## The shorter the e-mail message, the better.

Here is an e-mail I received responding to my voice-mail suggesting a 4:30 PM employment interview for an accounting position. The job applicant never tried to reach me by phone.

To: Marsha Egan
Subject: Re: Interview Request

Marsha,

I am sorry I did not get back to you sooner than 4 PM today. We implemented a couple new processes that were supposed to streamline the monthly accounting close. Both processes failed miserably on their first attempt, and I was at the office until 11:30 Monday night and did not receive your message until this morning. Unfortunately Thursday is horrible in terms of my schedule. I have various meetings scheduled throughout the day, and my spouse works in the afternoon and our babysitter is taking a class on Monday night so I have to watch my son starting at 5:30. I am unsure of your schedule but maybe we can arrange to meet somewhere around 4:30, I might be able to get away in time to meet you somewhere. Life is extremely busy for an accountant at the end/beginning of a month. My cell phone is actually on its last leg, and I ordered a new one that is coming via overnight delivery, but you may try and contact me on that (xxx) xxx-xxx if you wish. I carry it with me almost all the time, even though it does not work properly.

Regards, Velma

What conclusions can be drawn about this applicant's e-mail use and orientation? Are these kinds of e-mail messages toxic or helpful? This simple message would have been much more effective:

> "Marsha, that date is not convenient for me. These are the times I am available to meet with you: xxx, xxx"

Here's another...

See if you can easily determine the main request of this well intended e-mail communication:

> "Hi, Marsha! I am the xxx Director for the Albuquerque Chapter of the xxx and I visited your booth at our regional conference last year in Las Vegas. I've also enjoyed and received your e-newsletters and look forward to receiving them.
>
> I am also a member of the Editorial Committee for the xxx Magazine, our quarterly membership magazine. Our spring issue focus will be "Coaching" and I thought you would be a great resource for an article. We want to include a questionnaire to determine whether you need a coach - and I told the rest of the committee members that you might be able to help us with this. Would you have such a list available? Would you have an article that we might reprint in the magazine or would you be able to write an article on Coaching and how to determine whether coaching is an option for you?

I would love to hear back from you later today or tomorrow on if you could help us out. Xxx Smith, our magazine editor, will need to know your response by tomorrow. If you could e-mail me with your response, that would be most appreciated.

I look forward to seeing you at our upcoming regional meeting, and plan to stop by your booth."

What was the request? What was the action desired? How much time did it take to figure it out?

A better first sentence could have been:

"Marsha, we would love to have you write an article for our xxx publication and will need to know by tomorrow if you are interested."

(Background information follows)

Toxic E-mailer Alert

VERBOSE VELMA

Verbose Velma's e-mails run on and on and on and on and on and on...

Velma's Antidote: *Shorten the message, Velma! Her rule of thumb should be that if it will take longer to type her e-mail than to pick up the phone or visit the person and simply relay the message through conversation, don't waste time creating the e-mail message. Rather, call or visit, explain the situation, and if a record is needed, summarize it later by e-mail. That summary e-mail will be shorter than the originally intended one. In the long run, it will take Velma less time, and bring you better results.*

WRITE VERY SPECIFIC SUBJECT LINES

By incorporating detail into your subject lines, you enable the recipient to more easily sort, categorize, prioritize and file your message. "Please bring the attached handout to the Tuesday, 2/10 staff meeting" is much more precise and effective than "Staff Meeting."

Other examples include:

Subject: Request permission to reprint your xxx magazine article.

Subject: Driving directions for off-site meeting

Subject: Recommendation to change benefits provider to XYZ Company

95

As an added benefit, when the recipient responds, you can identify it and prioritize it immediately.

EOM: USE THE SUBJECT LINE AS THE ENTIRE MESSAGE

Sometimes, the entire brief message can be in the subject line. By placing "EOM" (abbreviation for End Of Message) at the end of the subject line, the reader will know that there is no need to open the e-mail.

Examples include:

Subject: Mary called in sick today. She has the flu. EOM

Subject: Support Services called. Your photocopies for the 8/23 presentation are available for pickup. EOM

Subject: We have cancelled the 1/20 staff meeting. EOM

CLEAN UP FORWARDED E-MAILS

When forwarding multiple appended e-mails, either highlight the key points to which you are referring or delete the extraneous information. This is a very respectful action that is extremely efficient, will minimize misunderstandings, and will save the recipient(s) extra time.

We have all groaned upon seeing lengthy forwarded e-mails, with simply "see below" as the message. How will the recipients know which part of which e-mail was important?

By noting, succinctly, the main point of the forwarded item—again, in the first two sentences of the e-mail—you will focus your reader's attention and honor their precious time.

Here is a well forwarded e-mail:

Hi Harry,
Below is Sandy's documentation for our new procedure. I highlighted the 3 main points in yellow.
Gilbert

Toxic E-mailer Alert

FORWARDING FRANK

Forwarding Frank forwards e-mails indiscriminately without editing or explaining the forward.

Frank's Antidote: *By taking just seconds to "clean up" the forwarded e-mails, and highlighting or even summarizing the most important points, Frank will save his readers time and confusion. Even more so, he may save himself from unnecessary return e-mails with questions asking for clarification.*

STOP THE EXPANDING THREADS

There are times when the best action is to stop the e-mails and refocus the respondents. Either call a meeting, or assign responsibility.

Some e-mail strings develop lives of their own. With multiple "reply alls" developing different strains, recipients may find exponentially growing numbers of e-mail messages on the same subject in their inboxes. These become increasingly difficult to determine who said what and when, and can require people to read and reread numerous e-mails.

The best action is to take control, and either summarily resolve the issue or call a meeting. Once the message has gone back and forth two or more times, the time spent handling it for each recipient increases as its effectiveness diminishes.

COPY ONLY THOSE WHO ABSOLUTELY NEED THE INFORMATION

How many times have you copied or blind copied a co-worker on an e-mail even if the person didn't necessarily need to have the information? Perhaps you did this in an effort to include the employee "just in case" he or she might like to know what's happening. Just to be "safe?"

Each time you add an extra five or ten people to your list of recipients "just to make sure no one is left out," you've forced those people to read an e-mail they really didn't need or want to read.

Not only is this practice absolutely unnecessary, but it also creates extra work for others in and outside of your organization. When an employee becomes accustomed to copying everyone under the sun, the multiplier effect soon takes over the organization, resulting in unnecessary time spent going back and forth with information.

Remember that when people receive an e-mail, they don't know whether they were the copied afterthought or an important recipient. So, they feel compelled to read the e-mail just as if they were a high priority recipient. And, most likely, they will respond, creating another e-mail for the "copy happy" worker. The situation becomes even worse when the responders reply to all, which is more the practice than the exception.

Toxic E-mailer Alert

COPY HAPPY HARRY

Harry loves e-mail. It is fast, inexpensive, and he can add anyone and everyone who might have even a smidge of interest in his topic or project, and it doesn't cost him a dime! So he does.

He has group lists, he has a huge database of...everyone. And he uses it. A lot.

Harry's Antidote: Harry should copy ONLY those people who really need to receive the information. Although Harry thinks this practice doesn't cost anything, it does. Every time a recipient has to open an unnecessary e-mail, it costs the company money. And most of them will respond to Harry, so it costs Harry more time.

USE THE TO: AND CC: LINES PROPERLY

Make sure that the person in the TO: line is the intended recipient of the message or assignment. Too many people place too many recipients in the TO: line. This practice is especially confusing when work is being assigned or questions are being asked, because the additional recipients may assume that others were intended to do the work, may reply asking to whom the assignment was directed, or will respond, feeling compelled to reply to all. Use the CC: line judiciously, and the BCC: line rarely.

> ## Too many people place too many recipients in the TO: line.

From: Phooey
To: Huey, Dooey, and Louie

Let's reserve the ABC Restaurant for our off site meeting, ok?
Phooey

Better...

From: Phooey
To: Huey
CC: Dooey and Louie

Huey, please reserve the ABC Restaurant from 5:00 – 9:30pm for our off site meeting, on January 25 ok?
Phooey

MISUSE OF THE BCC

Somewhat related to the copy happy e-mailer is the person who sends blind copies of e-mails to "interested" parties. This practice is akin to "playing rat." It can be viewed as tattling and its use as a valuable tool is questionable. If your organization is not open and trusting, the use of BCCs will evidence the symptom.

BCCs can be a source of awkwardness too. One of my clients lamented his using "Reply All" on an e-mail for which he received a BCC. At the time he responded, he didn't realize that he was "blind copied." The response caused recipients of his e-mail to raise questions as to how he got the e-mail, and destroyed the trust of the original e-mailer.

Toxic E-mailer Alert

BLIND COPY CALLIE

Callie uses her BCC whenever she wants management to know about an "issue." She uses the BCC to alert others to errors made by others, or as a way to provide inside information.

Callie's Antidote: While she thinks she is adding value, she isn't. Callie should deal with issues in the open.

USE "IF—THEN"

To cut down on the number of e-mails you receive, use the "if-then" approach. Include a statement with a qualifier that allows the recipient not to respond. By doing so, you can reduce the number of e-mails that both of you receive and send. Here are examples:

> Hi Sue,
> If the shipment of xxx has not been shipped, (then) please advise the planned ship date. If it has already shipped, no need to respond.

Or:

> Good morning, Jack,
> If you would like to set a tentative date for our workshop next month, please reply with suggested dates and times. If I don't hear from you, I will call you the first of the month when we have a better handle on our schedules.

On the other hand, avoid "what if" e-mails. "What if" e-mails essentially require a response either way. In the examples above, the "what if" e-mails would have read like this:

> Please advise the status of the xxx shipment.

Or:

> When would you like to schedule the workshop?

Remember, for every e-mail response you avoid, you will most likely save yourself 5 to 10 minutes.

AVOID LARGE SIZED E-STATIONERY

Many e-mail programs have the capability of selecting stationery that serves as a background for the e-mails you send. A multitude of these take large memory. Be very cautious about the use of these options as they can severely tax the capacity of both your system and systems of recipients.

USE PROPER BUSINESS LETTER WRITING PRACTICES

Many people are romanced into thinking that because of the informality of e-mail, they don't need to use proper grammar, punctuation or spelling. This is simply not true. When people read your e-mails, they draw conclusions about your professional abilities. A well written e-mail creates an excellent impression about your ability to communicate. Proper grammar, punctuation and spelling go a long way towards achieving your communication goals.

Take a small amount of time to proofread each e-mail message before you send it—this will help avoid follow up questions, and help position you as an excellent communicator.

Take a look at the following example—what's your impression?

From: Jacque
To: Lindy

Thx 4 the cntract. It is as we discuused. Am returninng it w/ signature in today's male w/ dnpmt.

Toxic E-mailer Alert

TEXT LINGO LULU

Lulu uses hip texting lingo in all her e-mails.

Here's one of her e-mails:

To: Henry
Fr: LuLu
R U here 2day or R U ooo?

(translation: Are you here today or are you out of office?)

While she may think text abbreviations are efficient, the reader may not know the "lingo," and worse, she's not managing her first impression very well.

LuLu's Antidote: *Don't do it LuLu! The risk of leaving a poor impression is not worth the time saved.*

By including your contact information in every sent e-mail, you make it easy for the recipient to respond to you, whether by e-mail, telephone, or post. Most e-mail programs have this feature. They also have the capability for you to program various auto signatures for you to use with different audiences. A standard default auto signature might look like this:

```
Clint
Clint Smith, Vice President
ABC Company
123 Park Road
Anywhere, PA, 19500
610-xxx-xxxx
TF: 877-xxx-xxxx
F: 610-xxx-xxxx
C: 610-xxx-xxxx
clint@abcco.com
www.abcco.com
```

Here's a bonus: many people like to add your contact information into their databases, and a full auto signature makes it easy for them to do so electronically.

BEWARE OF "FANCY" SIGNATURES

Some people attach JPEG files of logos or JPEG images of their handwritten signatures that, unless edited, can be a very large file size. If you choose to use these in your correspondence, make sure the file size has been reduced.

BEWARE THE VCARD

Some e-mail programs have the ability for you to attach your contact information in the form of an electronic business card. Known as the internet standard for sharing electronic business cards, the vCard or Versitcard, with a file extension of .vcf, enables the importing of contact information into various e-mail programs.

On first blush, this capability appears quite savvy. The efficiency concern is that some of these appear in others' inboxes as an e-mail with an attachment in some e-mail programs.

While you may think this is not significant, most people feel compelled to open the e-mail message when they see an attachment indicated, creating a potential unnecessary opening of the e-mail.

Note this comment from a vCard user:

vCards are deceiving... They make every e-mail appear as if it has an attachment. It does in one respect, but it's not what you would normally consider an attachment i.e. a document, a spreadsheet, etc.

And, here is another e-mailer's vCard experience:

I used to have a vcard on every e-mail that went out. I ended up getting blocked by hundreds of my clients' spam filters. I still am not able to get through to some of clients simply because of the v cards.

Many people manage their e-mail by using preview features available in their e-mail programs, and having to unnecessarily open an e-mail is just one more unwanted time waster.

USE VOTING BUTTONS

Most e-mail programs have a feature that allows recipients to respond using yes/no, accept/reject, yes/no/maybe, or custom designed voting buttons. This feature allows simple polling of a group, with electronic summaries supplied to the sender. This is just one of the efficiencies built into e-mail programs for our use.

Examples of efficient uses of this tool are to use e-mail voting options to ask whether the recipients plan to register for an upcoming conference, or whether they approve of a proposed procedure revision.

Caution: it is best not to use this feature to set up appointments, teleconferences, or meetings. There is a better method, discussed below.

USE THE CALENDAR FEATURE TO SCHEDULE APPOINTMENTS AND MEETINGS

Most e-mail programs have a "Calendar" feature that not only allows you to schedule important meetings and due dates, but also sends you reminders and prompts about those appointments you have docketed. By using the calendar feature, you can keep track of dates conveniently.

Even more importantly, when everyone in your work group consistently inputs all meetings and appointments in their electronic calendars, the calendar search feature makes finding open and convenient times to meet a snap. This tool allows users to view others' calendars to see when they are available, and make meeting requests that go directly into the calendars upon acceptance. Your calendar can and should also be used to block out the time in your schedule for your own projects, helping you to avoid scheduling conflicts with others. Doing so will save you valuable time, but only if everyone in the group enters every scheduled time on his or her calendar.

We have all been exasperated with the multiple e-mails back and forth, trying to find time for a simple meeting:

From: Elke
To: John; Ginger; Ezzat; Matt
Sent: November 9, 5:31 PM
Subject: RE: Budget Meeting

We need to meet to finalize the budget. Are you available next Tuesday at 2:00? Elke

---

From: John
To: Ginger; Ezzat; Matt; Elke
Sent: November 9, 5:41 PM
Subject: FW: Budget Meeting

Yes, it's in the book!
J

109

From: Ginger
To: Elke; Matt; John
Sent: November 10, 1:25 PM
Subject: RE: Budget Meeting

Yes, how long will the meeting last?
Ginger

From: Elke
To: Matt; Ginger
Sent: November 10, 3:21 PM
Subject: RE: Budget Meeting

You should plan two hours.

Thanks, Elke

From: Matt
To: Ginger; Elke; John
Sent: November 11, 10:16 AM
Subject: RE: Budget Meeting

I'm sorry, I'm not available after 3:00. Can we move it to 1:00?

Thanks! Matt

From: Ginger
To: Elke; Matt; John
Sent: November 11, 12:05 PM
Subject: RE: Budget Meeting

That works for me. Ginger

From: John
To: Ginger; Ezzat; Matt; Elke
Sent: November 11, 1:41 PM
Subject: FW: Budget Meeting

Me too. J

From: Elke
To: Tuesday, November 12, 3:21 PM
Sent: Matt; John; Ginger
Subject: RE: Budget Meeting

I can't do it at 1:00. What about Wednesday at 2? Elke

How much time do these unnecessary e-mails steal from each recipient's day?

Work groups who use the calendar feature can greatly increase their efficiency.

In my corporate career, after the leadership team became fed up with all the time it took to find time for meetings, we collectively decided to "mandate" the use of the electronic calendar to schedule meetings. Our department of 70+ people was given one week to enter all scheduled meetings into their electronic calendars. We then "required" that all meeting requests, even one-on-ones, be handled electronically. People remarked at how they "couldn't believe how easy and efficient it was!" Furthermore, those who initially forgot to schedule items on their calendars "learned" quickly after one or two instances of having to plea forgiveness from the rest of the group for a change of time.

Included in the electronic calendar tool in most e-mail programs is the ability to schedule a recurring meeting or an appointment, as in the case of a weekly staff meeting.

CONSIDER THE OVERALL TIME FOR THE TRANSACTION

When deciding whether to e-mail, call or visit, consider the overall transaction time of all parties involved, not just the amount of time it takes you to create and send your e-mail.

Here is another six e-mail discourse that will make you groan. A simple phone call would have handled it in minutes.

From: Kim
To: Bob
Sent: Tuesday, September 21, 5:01 PM
Subject: Discussion

Hi Bob - I'm BACK!

Time to discuss?

Thanks for your patience, Kim

From: Bob
To: Kim
Sent: Tuesday, September 21, 6:22 PM
Subject: RE: Discussion

How bout next Tues the 28th at 3 p.m.? bob

From: Kim
To: Bob
Sent: Wednesday, September 22, 9:18 AM
Subject: RE:RE: Discussion

Any chance earlier time?

From: Bob
To: Kim
Sent: Wednesday, September 22, 9:24 AM
Subject: RE:RE:RE: Discussion

yes, you give me the time and I'll put it in the book. This can be a phone call. Thanks. Bob

From: Kim
To: Bob
Sent: Wednesday, September 22, 9:25 AM
Subject: RE:RE:RE:RE: Discussion

OK - how is 2:00?

From: Bob
To: Kim
Sent: Wednesday, September 22, 9:37 AM
Subject: RE:RE:RE:RE:RE: Discussion

Fine, talk to you then. Bob

How much overall time would this transaction have taken if Kim had picked up the phone, or used her electronic calendar?

When I ask clients if they have ever e-mailed the person in the next cubicle or office, nine times out of ten, the answer is yes. Sometimes this practice is appropriate –

in the case of simple questions for which people don't want to interrupt or impose – but other times, it's absolutely ridiculous because the item requires discussion.

This practice isn't happening with only the person in the next cubicle, but applies to anyone within reasonable range of contact. Some people are said to hide behind their e-mail, using it prolifically even when other means of communication are more appropriate.

One of my teleseminar participants shared a similar situation he observed through being copied on a string of e-mails between a sales manager and a production manager. They were trying to arrange an office visit for an important client. After nine increasingly tense e-mails, ultimately intimating that the production manager had no sense of urgency about arranging the visit, one of them e-mailed the other, "I'm coming to your office so we can resolve." In one minute, she walked up one flight of stairs with her calendar, and the date was set. These e-mails had started three days prior. Obviously, their getting together at the outset could have resolved the question three days sooner, with collaboration rather than animosity.

Toxic E-mailer Alert

KEYBOARD KIM

Keyboard Kim's fingers are locked to her keyboard. That's all she does — tap away on those keys.

Kim's Antidote: *Kim should call or visit when discussion is needed. Many times, face-to-face or telephone discussion is much preferred over e-mail. Simply taking the initiative to meet with a person, and getting the issue resolved with dialogue will enable Kim to convey her facial expressions, body language, and feedback that can make an interaction more useful. Kim needs to remember, e-mail can never replace conversation.*

E-MAIL IS NOT A MEETING

Some people use e-mail to discuss issues and gain opinions. Each time an opinion question is sent to numerous people or to a group list, the e-mails tend to develop branches: the opinions multiply exponentially, the threads take on different paths, and each recipient is now receives multiple strings of the same subject e-mail that have gone in different directions. It all results in spending much more collective time than a one time meeting or teleconference may have taken. This makes it more difficult for participants to see the big picture and the overall opinions. The multiple threads are confusing and time consuming.

Instead of using e-mail this way, it is much more effective and productive to call a meeting and discuss the issue in detail. Invoke the two-round rule: when you see e-mails circling back the second time, call a meeting to discuss the issue in further detail and put an end to future lack of productivity caused by all those e-mails. Better yet, call the meeting in the first place.

Toxic E-mailer Alert

CHATROOM CHUCK

Chuck could sit behind his desk all day. He likes using group e-mails and e-mails to challenge numerous recipients to discuss issues. The more opinions, and the more responses to the responses. The threads multiply exponentially, and Chuck thrives on all the attention that his one e-mail created.

Chuck's Antidote: *E-mail should not be used as a chat room—that is, to discuss detailed and involved opinion questions among multiple recipients, or to build group consensus about key issues. Chuck needs to assess the most effective way to collect effective feedback in the shortest amount of time, rather than relying on e-mail to a large group.*

BE JUDICIOUS IN YOUR USE OF ATTACHMENTS

According to recent research by The Radicati Group, a major cause of the yearly cost of e-mail is attributable to e-mail attachments which make up more than 85% of all e-mail data.[7] Twenty percent of all e-mails contain attachments, but as much as 92% of e-mail resources are consumed by attachments, the same survey reported, and the average corporate e-mail user sent and received over 4MB of e-mail attachments per day.

Some attachments can be quite large, and can take a long time to download. Forwarding pictures and videos fall into this category. A good rule of thumb is "think before you attach."

SAVE LARGE ATTACHMENTS TO YOUR HARD DRIVE

You've got to be concerned about the size of your electronic files. If your e-mail system is too overloaded, it could slow or possibly crash. Therefore, when you have important attachments, especially ones that have a large file size, it can be helpful to save them to your hard drive.

Once again, the files on your hard drive should mirror your paper and e-mail files for ease of finding and categorizing items.

7 *"Messaging Total Cost of Ownership," The Radicati Group, Inc., Palo Alto, CA, August 2005.*

SAVE THE E-MAIL, BUT DELETE THE ATTACHMENT

To help you manage the size of your e-mail files, you may determine that you do not need the attachment, just the e-mail.

Sometimes when there are numerous e-mail messages related to the same subject or attachment, people end up with multiple copies of that same attachment in their e-mail folders. This presents a great opportunity to purge those extra attachments.

MANAGE YOUR E-MAIL WITH RULES

Many e-mail programs have rules that you can apply to received e-mail messages. In other words, you can set up a rule that routes a message automatically into one of your e-mail action folders without having it go into or through your inbox. An example is to set a rule to have e-newsletters routed directed into your Action – Reading folder.

By establishing rules that place e-mail messages directly into a folder, rather than requiring you to sort, drag, and drop, you can save more precious minutes.

USE PREVIEW PANE OR AUTO PREVIEW

To avoid having to open every e-mail, most e-mail programs allow you to set up your e-mail in preview pane view. This lets you see the content of roughly half a page of the e-mail without having to double-click on the e-mail to open it.

You can also use Auto Preview, which allows you to read the first three lines of all of the e-mails in your folders.

Remember, every minute or second you save will add up.

PURGE YOUR FOLDERS REGULARLY

To avoid overtaxing the resources of your e-mail program, it is important that you delete those e-mail messages and attachments that are no longer needed. You can apply the same system you use for purging your paper—some people review and purge their folders quarterly, or at regular intervals; others make it a practice to purge files and folders every time they are in those files.

SET YOUR E-MAIL PROGRAM TO PURGE DELETED ITEMS UPON CLOSE

Most e-mail programs have a feature whereby you can set up the program to purge all deleted items whenever you close the e-mail program. This will help you manage the size of your files, making it one less action you'll have to take.

PURGE YOUR SENT MAIL

One of the common system burdening oversights is not purging sent mail. Without regular purging, these folders can quickly grow to thousands of e-mails requiring extensive memory resources.

Periodically, make it a habit to review your sent mail, save the important ones to the proper reference files, save the needed attachments to your hard drive, and be done with it.

THE CAREER E-STRATEGY

Using e-mail best practices can truly enhance your productivity and effectiveness. Similarly, there are several e-mail blunders that can actually hurt you.

Every interaction you have with others inside and outside the workplace is an occasion to create an impression - positive, neutral or negative. Because of the frequency of e-mail "impressions," the quality, tone, and timing of your e-mail messages can impact opinions that can impede or enhance your career.

Here are some of the top saboteurs and how to avoid them.

EMOTIONAL CONTENT

There is a real risk to allowing emotion into e-mails. When e-mails are composed in an emotional state, your thinking may be clouded. Even though you may read and reread the message, you may not see it from the perspective of others who will read it.

123

It is widely understood that 70 percent to 80 percent of all face-to-face communication is done with voice inflection and body language. Therefore, only 20 to 30 percent of the message can get through via e-mail. No wonder arguments have started, tempers have flared, people have been hurt, suggestions have been misinterpreted —the list goes on and on—via the use (or misuse) of e-mail.

In fact, in the AOL survey, almost half of the respondents, 45 percent, indicated that they would like to have the ability to retrieve a message they have sent.[8]

Argumentative, emotional, or controversial e-mails should not be sent; it usually makes more sense to discuss any touchy, critical, or argumentative issues in person.

Here is an example of an e-mail message that might be interpreted in several ways:

> **From:** Jeff
> **To:** Mutt
> **Subject:** Comment
> ___
> You challenged me in today's meeting. I'll remember this.
> Jeff

___

8   Opinion   Research   Corp   Survey   for   AOL,   2006;
http://corp.aol.com/press-releases

Was Jeff pleased? Was he complementing Mutt? Was he angry? Was he threatening Mutt?

It is really important that the sender read and reread the e-mail before sending so that misinterpretation is minimized or avoided. That's why keeping e-mails simple and informational is a good habit to practice.

And if there is any doubt in the sender's mind, the best practice is to NOT send the message.

Toxic E-mailer Alert

EMOTIONAL EVAN

Evan gets upset easily. When he gets upset, he bangs on his keyboard. Evan sends e-mails that unintentionally upset others and tear down relationships.

Evan's Antidote: *Evan should send informational e-mails, not emotional ones. If angry or upset, Evan should wait till he cools off to compose the e-mail, or decide if it is even necessary. If he suspects that his emotions may have tarnished the message, he should sleep on it. If he still has doubts, he shouldn't send the e-mail. He should either let the issue go or consider handling the issue with a meeting or phone call.*

USING BUSINESS PROPERTY FOR PERSONAL REASONS

Accessing your home e-mail, checking your eBay listing, or conducting personal business on your employer's technology is a big no no.

Many employees make the mistake of using their business e-mail for personal reasons. Whether it's e-mailing the babysitter to check on the kids or keeping up with college buddies, personal e-mails are scarcely warranted from your workplace e-mail account.

A word to the wise: your employer owns your work e-mail account, and has a legal right to every piece of information transmitted over its business network. Even if deleted, sent e-mails can be "mined." In addition, remember that e-mails can constitute a public record; this is yet another reason not to use them to transmit sensitive, argumentative, or personal information from your work account. Even merely accessing your personal e-mail through your business's Internet system can be dangerous to your career, as records and logs of those transactions can be accessed by the company.

Some companies allow the occasional use of company technology for personal reasons. Others don't. If you have any doubt, check your company's Internet and e-mail use policies.

Toxic E-mailer Alert

PERSONAL PENELOPE

Penelope checks her home e-mail account regularly, and uses the company e-mail for personal things.

Penelope's Antidote: *Penelope should not do it. Period.*

APPEARING OBSESSIVE

It is career savvy to manage the impressions you make. Your e-mailing practices can help or hurt others' opinions of you. E-mailing at 3:00 in the morning is just one of these behaviors. Checking the PDA incessantly and in odd circumstances is another.

Have you ever received an e-mail sent at 3:30 am? What did you think of the e-mailer? Was it positive?

Some employees actually think they will impress their bosses and co-workers by sending e-mails while others are sleeping. Most people do not view this practice positively. It raises questions about one's inability to sleep: is this person running on all cylinders at 3 o'clock in the morning; and why is he or she obsessing about this anyway?

MIDNIGHT MANNY

Manny sends e-mails in the middle of the night. Regularly.

Manny's Antidote: *Manny needs to be very cautious about this practice. First, he may be sleep deprived and not in full control of his reasoning. And second, just as important as managing his work, it is important for him to manage the impressions he sends. Even if he is one of those rare folks who does his best work in these off hours, he can't control what others think.*

USING E-MAIL TO CRITICIZE OR DISCIPLINE

When e-mail is used to provide "constructive" criticism, or to discipline, the message will most likely be snowballed, misinterpreted, and yes, kept as "evidence" against you. E-mails can be copied. They can be saved. And they can be forwarded. Especially if you are in the habit of using e-mail in this way, the evidence can, and will mount. All of a sudden, you'll be the one hauled into HR.

How would you feel if you received the following e-mail?

From: Dixie
To: Mica

I was very pleased with your slide presentation today.

One small bit of advice: please make sure you spell check your entire presentation in advance, I counted at least five spelling errors in your 32 slide presentation.

Please accept this in a friendly helpful tone it was meant. Dixie

E-mail is very easily misinterpreted. When you use e-mail to discipline, reprimand, criticize, or to "be helpful," chances are that the recipient won't receive it in the way you meant it. You open the door to a multitude of e-mails in reply. Or worse, covert feelings of hurt, disappointment, and even revenge.

Though it may seem like a fast and productive way to deal with the issue, e-mail criticism can prompt a myriad of e-mails back and forth, involving many more people than necessary. In addition, the trail of e-mails can leave a written record of the transaction, which may work to be detrimental to the e-mailer or the company in the future.

The best practice has always been to reward in public, and discipline in private. E-mail is not the proper tool for private criticism or feedback.

129

DISCIPLINING DIXIE

Dixie disciplines and critiques by e-mail.

Dixie's Antidote: Because of the possibility of misunder-standing or miscommunication, as well as a lack of face-to-face interaction, Dixie needs to understand that e-mail is not appropriate for disciplining co-workers or pointing fingers at wrongdoers. She will be much more effective when she provides feedback in person.

PLAYING E-MAIL "GOTCHA"

A similar reaction is reached when e-mailers "throw people under the bus," informing a co-worker that he or she has made a mistake, and copying several others. These kinds of e-mails make their recipients—particularly those who are accused of committing an error —likely to respond defensively. And because others are copied, the recipient will feel compelled to respond to every named recipient or person involved. Feeling like they are standing in front of an e-mail jury, they feel compelled to defend themselves. All of this creates additional e-mail traffic that is rarely useful.

Worse, it gives the impression that you're not a team player, untrustworthy, a tattle tale, and out for yourself at someone else's expense.

Finally, these e-mails can be copied and forwarded. Bosses don't appreciate tattle tails. That memo could land in YOUR file.

> **Toxic E-mailer Alert**
>
> ## GOTCHA GARY
>
> *Gary is a rat. Whenever he learns that someone has messed up, he calls them on it, publicly, via e-mail. He copies everyone he can. He "wins" at the expense of the victim.*
>
> ***Gary's Antidote:*** *Gary shouldn't even think of doing it. If he wants to give feedback, he should give it individually, respectfully, and in person to only the person he is trying to help.*

BEHIND THE BACK "GOTCHA"

Creating controversy by e-mail can be destructive too. This is like playing "gotcha" without including the victim in the distribution. Again, because so much can be misinterpreted, what may start as a simple controversy could actually create more work, more hard feelings, and ultimately require more time to smooth out any issues that result.

And sometimes it is not so innocent. Back stabbing by e-mail exists, and can be even more career threatening to the sender than confronting the "victim" and copying others. It is sneaky, it is unfair, it is intentional, and creates negativity — and most people see it that way.

Consider the following example:

From: Tinman
To: Dorothy, Scarecrow
Subject: Staff Meeting

Hi D & S- What did you think of Lion's behavior in the meeting today? I can't believe that he didn't have the courage to stand up for his proposal. After all, that's all he's talked about in the last few weeks. I think we should let the boss know, don't you? It makes all of us look bad, don't you agree?

Tinman

Toxic E-mailer Alert

CONTROVERSIAL CONNIE

Connie uses e-mail to stir the pot. She criticizes others by e-mail without including them in the distribution.

Connie's Antidote: *Connie should avoid sending any e-mails that may hurt a co-worker. This is where face-to-face interaction is the outwardly honest approach.*

SLOPPY WRITING, PUNCTUATION, SPELLING, OR GRAMMAR

Managing your impression is a key career strategy. People draw conclusions about you every time they interact with you. Because e-mail is so pervasive, the quality of your message writing can help or hurt your career.

According to an October 2005 survey by Information Mapping, Inc., 80 percent of those surveyed deemed e-mail writing skills "extremely" or "very" important to the effectiveness of doing their jobs. Approximately 65 percent of the respondents spent from one to three hours per day reading and writing e-mails, with 40 percent claiming to waste 30 minutes to three hours reading "ineffectively" written e-mails.[9] On that note, read e-mails carefully. Here is an example of a misread e-mail that created extra work and correspondence. Have you ever received an e-mail like this one?

From: Marsha
To: Curly
Sent: Friday, June 15
Subject: RE: 6/14 Orlando, FL Itinerary

Hi Curly,
Do I send my expenses to you or to Mo?
Thanks! Marsha

9 *"Ineffective Business Communications," Information Mapping, Inc., Waltham, MA, October 2005.*

From: Curly
To: 'Marsha Egan'
Sent: Monday, June 18, 9:10 AM
Subject: RE: 6/14 Orlando, FL Itinerary

Hi Marsha,
Yes, that would be great.
Thanks! Curly

From: Marsha
To: Curly
Sent: Monday, June 18, 10:10 AM
Subject: RE: 6/14 Orlando, FL Itinerary

To you or to Mo?
Thanks! Marsha

From: Marsha
To: Curly
Sent: Monday, June 18, 10:32 AM
Subject: RE: 6/14 Orlando, FL Itinerary

I'm sorry. Please send them to Mo.

VIEWING AND E-MAILING FROM YOUR PDA DURING MEETINGS

Working your portable e-mail during a meeting can have severe career limiting consequences. We have all met the co-worker, or even the boss, who not only places the PDA on the meeting table, but checks it periodically.

According to a survey by Robert Half Management Resources, who surveyed 150 Fortune 1000 senior executives[10], 86 percent said it was common for their coworkers to read and respond to e-mail during meetings. 54 percent of those senior executives frowned upon the practice; 31 percent flat-out disapproved; and another 23 percent said coworkers should excuse themselves from the meeting when handling e-mail, the same survey reported.

With over half of the executives in the survey disapproving of the practice, you've got a one in two chance that your career can be impacted. Do you want those odds?

Focusing on the Blackberry, or even placing it on the meeting or dining table, sends the strong signal that it has more value than the subject at hand. This behavior can be viewed as insulting and as evidence that your priorities are confused.

---

10 *Robert Half Management Resources, Menlo Park, April, 2007*

THE ECO-FRIENDLY HABIT

Healthy e-mail habits include those that are healthy for the environment.

It is no secret that the amount of paper consumption has increased since the advent of computer automation. And even though the paperless office was supposed to lead to the demise of paper, in many areas it has actually led to notable increases. E-mail has significantly impacted the earth's carbon footprint — a never intended consequence.

Just think of how you treat your e-mail... even though it is electronic and can be read and responded to electronically, many people print and file those e-mails. What about you? How many times and day do you print an e-mail or its attachments? Do you do it consciously, or out of habit?

Just think of the impact on the world's paper consumption if everyone would print 50 percent fewer e-mails and their attachments in only one day. Just think of the impact if it was done every day!

WHY DO PEOPLE PRINT SO MUCH?

Why do people print so many messages that could be stored and retrieved electronically? Much of it stems from psychological, aesthetic, habitual, and legal reasons. Here are some of them:

- · You like to touch and hold the information.
- · You like to flip pages back and forth.
- · You like to write comments, and make notes.
- · You like to physically file items for reference.
- · You take information with you to meetings.
- · You need them for legal reasons.

While some of the above reasons justify the printing of documents, there are electronic means to achieve similar results. Some of these involve the breaking of old comfortable habits, others require a shift in the way you handle your work.

Let's review each of these "justifications" for printing e-mail messages:

"Liking" to touch the paper

Many people find comfort in holding on to a document while reading it. As for touching and holding the information, while it may be comfortable or familiar, our technology enables us otherwise. It is entirely possible to read just about anything on a computer screen without having to print it. There is an environmental cost for this comfort. The big question could be are you caring more about your own needs than those of the environment?

"Liking" to flip pages and make notes

As for the ability to flip pages back and forth, annotate items, highlight important phrases and view more than one page at a time, all of these can be done electronically.

"Liking" to edit

Again, our habits can get in the way. We've been conditioned to edit on a paper document. Electronic documents are easier to edit, and even easier to show what was added, deleted, or modified by multiple contributors.

"Liking" to physically file items for reference

Once again, these are conditioned habits. Electronic folders are easier to source, less cumbersome to maintain, more searchable, and more space saving.

"Liking" to carry it with you

Paper enables the portability of information. Needing to carry documents with you to meetings for reference may be a legitimate reason for printing. Then again, it may be "old school." The challenge here is to use as little paper as possible, and only what is needed. Some PDAs enable you to carry that information with you electronically.

Legal documentation

Regarding the need for legal documentation, there may be very legitimate reasons for the printing of these documents. However, more and more, electronic documents are being accepted as legal documentation, so check your state laws and print the least amount possible.

PAPER SAVING PRACTICES

Paper saving practices you can consider are:

- Print only what you need.
- Don't automatically print all pages of a document without reviewing the entire document and selecting only what you need.
- If you need only a brief item of information, make a note of it in your PDA or planner.
- Make wider margins and single space documents when possible.
- When printing, print two pages to a page.
- File electronically.
- Use both sides of the paper.
- Use the "track changes" feature to edit and comment on documents.
- Add "Please consider the environment before printing this e-mail" to your e-mail auto signature.

140

The most important practice is to "think before you print."

Even though trees are a renewable resource, the fewer we have to renew, the better for the environment. Set a goal to print as few items as possible, and at least 50% less than what you print in a normal day. Just think of the compound impact! And make it a habit.

> ## Think before you print.

BUT THERE'S MORE...

You can have all the policies and good habits in the world, avoid all career blunders, and save a lot of paper, but if you fail to convey and project respect for your recipients, you may still come off as an e-buffoon. The next chapter addresses the proper use of etiquette in e-mails, projecting respect through savvy e-communication habits.

THE ETIQUETTE HABIT

In discussing effective e-mail habits, e-mail etiquette takes positive e-mail habits to the highest level. A truly sophisticated e-mailer projects professionalism by his or her consistent use of proper e-mail etiquette.

Etiquette is based on respect. Any book on the subject of positive and proactive e-mail practices would be remiss in not reminding the reader of the appropriate etiquette for this communication tool.

Here are the basics of e-mail etiquette that will consistently enhance your image and productivity once they've become engrained habits.

USE SENTENCE CASE

If you use ALL CAPS, IT APPEARS AS IF YOU ARE SHOUTING. No one wants to be shouted at; to avoid this misimpression, always use upper and lower case, commonly known as "sentence case." And while using sentence case appears to be a common understanding

143

among regular e-mail users, there are some people who still are unaware of the poor impression ALL CAPS creates.

Take a look at these examples:

From: Helmut
To: Allison

I was wondering when you will be able to send me the accounting figures we discussed... Please advise.

From: Helmut
To: Allison

I was wondering WHEN you will be able to send me the accounting figures we discussed... PLEASE ADVISE.

The same rule applies to avoiding using all lower case: doing so can give the impression that you are lazy. How does the next example appear to you?

From: Helmut
To: Allison

i was wondering when you will be able to send me the accounting figures we discussed... please advise.

PERSONALIZE THE MESSAGE

This practice could be the easiest and most effective etiquette practice. By incorporating the person's first name in to the body of the e-mail, you will go a long way in showing respect. A simple greeting—for instance, "Dear Donna," Good morning, Harry," or "It was nice to hear from you, Pat"—can show great e-mail etiquette in a matter of seconds.

Remember, everyone loves to hear (or see) their name.

DO NOT SHARE LARGE LISTS OF E-MAIL ADDRESSES VIA CC

Placing a large number of e-mail addresses of recipients who don't know each other in the CC shares private information with many recipients. Indiscriminate copying can actually be viewed as an invasion of privacy.

Instead, either enter the e-mail addresses in the BCC line or use the mail merge feature.

BEWARE THE USE OF THE BCC

Your use of the BCC option could be interpreted as backstabbing, end runs, or mistrust. Consider this e-mail (bold emphasis added) blind copied to "the boss:"

From: Howdy
To: Doodie
BCC: Boss Bob
Sent: January 19, 2:41 PM
Subject: 4th Quarter Training Report

Good morning, Doodie;
When do you plan to submit your 4th Quarter Training Report?

It was due the 15th, and this is now my third follow-up. I've received the reports from all other managers, and will appreciate your getting the information to me ASAP.

Thanks.
Howdy

Before you use this feature, think about the reasons you are really considering doing so, and determine whether the use is truly necessary. Consider also how its use might make you look to other recipients. In the above example, it is plain to the BCC recipient that Howdy is "tattling" to Boss Bob. Very disrespectful. Very poor etiquette.

WHEN THE BCC IS OK

One exception to the BCC caution noted above is when you're sending a mass e-mail, such as a Rotary Club meeting announcement, to people who may not know each other. In distributions like this, it is best to put their e-mail addresses in the BCC line. This keeps others from "mining" the e-mail addresses that appear to everyone in the TO or CC lines.

REMEMBER: THE RECIPIENT CANNOT HEAR YOUR TONE

When crafting an e-mail message, always keep in mind that the receiver cannot hear your tone of voice or notice your body language. Be aware of the potential for misinterpretation, and create your message with the recipient in mind. By re-reading, you may be able to avoid misinterpretations.

From: Fred
To: Ginger
Sent: August 23, 8:16 AM
Subject: Dance Practice

I told you to smile at the audience when I twirl you around…

Did he mean:

- I TOLD you to smile at the audience when I twirl you around… (I told ya so)

- I told YOU to smile at the audience when I twirl you around… (I wasn't telling someone else, I was telling you)

- I told you to SMILE at the audience when I twirl you around… (You were frowning, you should smile)

- I told you to smile AT THE AUDIENCE when I twirl you around... (Don't smile at me, smile at the audience)

- I told you to smile at the audience when I twirl YOU around... (The time to smile is during the twirl)

OR... was he just flirting in a funny way??? Hmmmm...

Just remember, e-mail can not be equated to conversation. E-mail presents information in one dump, without any feedback. You can not see the body language that allows you to "read" the recipient, adjust your tone or respond differently. That is why it is unfortunately misread and misinterpreted regularly.

AVOID EMOTICONS, ABBREVIATIONS, AND SMILEY FACES

While some of these may be cute, there is little need for them in a business environment. Emoticons sent via a business e-mail can paint an employee as puerile and unprofessional. Smiley faces should be left for personal e-mailing. In addition, unknown abbreviations can cause confusion.

For instance, do you understand the following message?

> **From:** Howard
> **To:** Betty
> **Sent:** February 23, 11:16 AM
> **Subject:** F2F Mtg Req
>
> Am req a F2F w/ u ITNF, 2 discuss upcoming PRs. R U available Mon @ 3? Pls lv a msg on my vm, as I w/b OOO. L8R, H

Translation: Face to face Meeting Request

I am requesting a face-to-face meeting with you in the near future to discuss upcoming performance reviews. Are you available Monday at 3:00? Please leave a message on my voice mail, as I will be out of the office. Later, Howard

While some common and universally understood abbreviations—such as FYI (For Your Information) and EOM (End Of Message)—can be appropriate, others, like BTW (By The Way,) and TTFN (Ta Ta For Now) may be confusing. They may even prompt a needless return e-mail by the recipient asking what they mean.

ALWAYS CONSIDER THE RECIPIENT

Many etiquette blunders can be avoided by simply considering your recipient(s) and trying to "receive" the message from their eyes. There aren't enough etiquette rules to account for every situation, so consider the perspective of each recipient every time you send an e-mail.

Have you ever saved business e-mails from the previous week and sacrificed the weekend to handle them? If so, you probably felt like you were efficient and committed, figuring you were contributing to the organization's productivity by using your precious personal weekend time taking care of business. You're not alone: research shows that Saturdays and Sundays account for the highest percentage of "open and click" rates by e-mail users.[11]

In fact, when business e-mails are saved for weekend handling, it creates a huge e-mail bubble among the Monday morning recipients. People who think that they are giving more to the company by committing weekend time to catch up on their e-mail may actually be creating more challenges for their co-workers.

I worked for a boss who was a "weekend warrior." Frankly, I couldn't stand the thought of going to work on Monday morning. Before I arrived at the office, I knew I would have a minimum of 30, sometimes up to 50 e-mails from my boss. These were items that I could have managed the prior week, and some of them became unnecessarily urgent because he sat on them. It severely impacted all of his direct reports' abilities to manage their workloads. Mondays were relabeled as "Stress-days." We finally got together with him and convinced him to spread things out. What a difference that made!

---

11 See "Q2 2006 E-mail Statistics: Breaking Down E-mail Behaviors and Trends" by eRoi, Inc., 2006.

150

Toxic E-mailer Alert

WEEKEND WENDELL

Wendell uses every weekend to "catch up" with his large e-mail backlog.

Wendell's Antidote: *Instead of handling e-mails in one lump, he will do much better to space them out, adding e-mail management to his daily to-do list and building in systematic times to take care of e-mails.*

SAVE THE JOKES FOR YOUR PERSONAL E-MAIL

We all know the person who continually shares many jokes daily with his or her group list. Most people "ugh" when they see these come through, especially when they're trying to sift through their 100 other e-mails.

With so many people getting so much e-mail in their business day, the last thing colleagues and others need is another e-mail to open and to read. Rest assured that when your coworkers access their personal e-mail accounts, they will find enough uplifting jokes and inspirational messages there. Respect your recipient, and respect your business: stop with the personal stuff!

I can almost hear the groans when people open and read either a joke or an inspirational message that closes with the usual "Send this to 10 extraordinary human beings within the next 24 hours, or else..."

One of the frequent questions we receive from clients has to do with e-mail jokes and forwarded messages. "How can you tell one of your dearest friends that you really don't need to see the jokes or inspirational messages they send daily to their ever growing group joke list? You surely don't want to hurt the person or lose a friend."

Here is one suggestion. Remember, the issue is best handled in person rather than by e-mail. Find a time when you are having a friendly conversation either in person or over the telephone, because an e-mail will most likely be hurtful. Be direct; say "it would be great if you could send me only your very best e-mails, because I am inundated with e-mail, though I could definitely use an uplifting message once or twice a week."

Another solution is to create a separate personal joke e-mail account, i.e. JonsJokes@gmail.com, and ask your joking friends to send all future jokes to that account. You can then access it when you need a laugh, rather than to have to deal with it as part of your business inbox.

Toxic E-mailer Alert

JOKING JON

Joking Jon loves jokes and scours the internet for the latest and greatest. He has an ever growing e-mail group to whom he sends at least 2 GREAT jokes every day.

Jon's Antidote: *Jon should never send jokes to business e-mail addresses. He should also read, research and send jokes only on his personal time.*

FOLLOW "THE GOLDEN RULE"

Following the "Golden Rule" applies just as much in e-mail transactions as in other life situations. By embracing the concept that you should treat your recipients the way you want to be treated, your e-mail transactions will bring fruitful and productive returns.

So, as you consider whether to send an e-mail, compose a message, or respond to a message, ask yourself how you would react upon receiving the communication.

'IF YOU DON'T' FRED

Fred sends those inspirational e-mails that threaten bad karma, give seven years' bad luck, or worse if the recipient fails to forward to 25 people in the next 20 seconds.

These "if you don't" messages may seem inspirational or funny to Fred. If Fred only knew how many people see them as not only threatening and insulting, but just plain annoying!

Fred's Antidote: *Fred shouldn't do it. Or, if the message is really valuable, Fred should delete the forwarding "threat!"*

For recipients and senders alike, a little bit of e-mail etiquette can go a long way. By using proper etiquette, you will look professional and polished.

Now that we've discussed inbox management, e-mail best practices, career limiting e-mails, eco-friendly e-mailing and etiquette, let's take a look at how we transition these tools to be long term useful habits.

THE ACKNOWLEDGEMENT

BEFORE WE CAN CREATE LASTING CHANGE...

Before we can create lasting change, we need to choose the practices we want to change. We've given you several resources to help you identify them, and here is the place to acknowledge them and bring them together.

One final resource can be the toxic e-mailers you've met throughout this book. Take one last look at them.

Are any of these toxic e-mailers familiar to you? How about VERY familiar? Take a quick moment to reflect on whether YOU have ever played any of these characters, and to what extent? 0=Never, 5=That's me to a T!

THE ACKNOWLEDGEMENT

CHARACTER	RATING
E-coward Ethan	
Double Checking Dilly	
Urgent Ursula	
Thankful Thelma	
Burier Bob	
Verbose Velma	
Forwarding Frank	
Copy Happy Harry	
Blind Copy Callie	
Text Lingo LuLu	
Keyboard Kim	
Chatroom Chuck	
Emotional Evan	
Personal Penelope	
Midnight Manny	
Disciplining Dixie	
Gotcha Gary	
Controversial Connie	
Weekend Wendell	
Joking Jon	
If You Don't Fred	
TOTAL	

Any score over 0 means you have potential to reclaim time and effectiveness. The higher the number, the more opportunity to improve!

These characters are a light way to draw your attention to some of the toxic e-mail sending practices that can sap your productivity. While you may recognize some of these traits in others, your ability to cure your own toxic habits will go far in helping you reclaim minutes hours and days for what is truly important to you.

THE TRANSFORMATION

HABITS ARE HARD TO BREAK

How can you transform these healthy practices into habits you keep?

In order to regain your personal productivity at work and at home, you must work consciously towards changing your e-mail habits and practices. The previous section showed you the methods; now, it's time to motivate yourself towards shifting those e-habits for the better. Once you commit to change and begin implementing better e-mail practices, you will not only gain valuable hours in your day, but also pry yourself free from being a slave to your e-mail.

After a recent seminar, one of my clients came up to me and groaned, "These concepts are so, so simple! Why are they so difficult?"

> # These concepts are so, so simple!
> # Why are they so difficult?

The answer is because they involve shifting habits.

A habit, by definition, is an acquired behavior pattern that has become almost involuntary as a result of frequent repetition.[11] Through acquiring habits, your attitudes toward the behavior become engrained. Because of the frequency of repetition, the way you handle your e-mail is most likely a habitual behavior. And to change those habits, you need to make an active choice to do so, first in your attitude, then your behavior.

CHANGE IS TOUGH

There is no denying that change is tough. Changing habits is even tougher.

Anyone who's ever attempted to give up an unhealthy habit or engrain a healthy one can attest to the difficulty involved in changing one's tried-and-true patterns and practices. For many, change — any change — can be a difficult task to face.

---

11 habit. (n.d.). Dictionary.com Unabridged (v 1.1). Retrieved July 14, 2007, from Dictionary.com website: http://dictionary.reference.com/browse/habit

"Change has considerable psychological impact on the human mind," said business executive King Whitney, Jr.[12] "To the fearful it is threatening because it means that things may get worse. To the hopeful it is encouraging because things may get better. To the confident it is inspiring because the challenge exists to make things better. Obviously, then, one's character and frame of mind determine how readily he brings about change and how he reacts to change that is imposed on him."

There are many reasons why people are fearful or apprehensive about change. For starters, some may not see or appreciate the need for change, wrongly believing that few or no complaints about the status quo mean change is not necessary. Others fear losing control or power as changes are implemented. Still others simply fear the aftermath of change, apprehensive about the possibility that the changed circumstances will bring about even more challenges in their environments.

As you take on the initiative to change your e-mail habits, having the answers to these questions in front of you will form your foundation for change. They will be the bedrock to help you maintain and press on, focusing on the behavior changes that will become your new, optimally productive e-mail habits.

One of my clients posted a note on her computer that read "One more hour a day!" This note served as her

---

12 As quoted in The Wall Street Journal, 7 June 67.

reminder to keep employing e-mail best practices whenever she felt drawn back to her old e-mail habits. The thought of finding an extra hour each day was a powerful trigger thought which helped her refocus on the ultimate goal of reclaiming time for what is truly important to her.

ADOPT NEW HABITS

"You form habit patterns in your subconscious mind by repeating a thought or act over and over until it establishes tracks in the subconscious mind and becomes automatic," describes Dr. Joseph Murphy, author of *The Power of Your Subconscious Mind.*[13]

We all know people who have dieted and lost 30 pounds, only to gain it all back again. The reason? They changed their practices only temporarily. To keep the weight off, they needed to shift their eating habits permanently, but unfortunately they didn't. Applying this example to our e-mail practices, we need to commit to shifting those practices and engraining them in our daily routines for the long-term future.

It's been said that it takes 21 days to change a habit. There has been a lot of discussion over whether this statement is true. What we do know is that it takes focused, active, and repetitive attention to change any engrained habit. And given that a shift in your subcon-

---

13 *Joseph Murphy, The Power of Your Subconscious Mind, Wilder Publications, 2008, p 275*

scious mind supports that effort, we suggest that you commit to at least a month of focus on replacing e-mail habits that don't serve you well with those that do. A month of Inbox Detox.

> ## It takes focused, active, and repetitive attention to change any engrained habit.

There is a difference between a change and a shift. Someone who diets for 3 months and loses 20 pounds changed how he or she ate for those 3 months. If new eating habits were "shifted," the weight will stay off. If the "old ways" of eating are resumed at the end of the diet, and those 30 pounds will return in a few months, the eating habits were merely changed for those 12 weeks. They did not "shift."

One of my seminar attendees was highly motivated to empty his inbox, and spent the weekend after the seminar doing so. He e-mailed me that Monday morning, proudly proclaiming that his inbox was empty. Three weeks later his inbox was back to the 300+ messages—about the same number he had only three weeks earlier. Did he change or *shift* his e-mail handling?

Another attendee commented, "Gee, this sure isn't rocket science! My biggest challenge will be remembering to do each of these simple steps, every day, every hour."

So, will you commit to adopting new habits?

SHIFT YOUR THINKING

Before you can expect to see any Inbox Detox results, you must change the way you think about e-mail. Remember, your thoughts and attitudes drive your actions. For example, you have to change the way you think about the inbox. Rather than allowing it to serve as a holding tank, you can view it as a receiving tool. You also can shift from viewing e-mail as an urgent communication tool to viewing it as a convenient communication tool.

If you believe that you must be constantly available to receive e-mail, then you will be tied to your desk or your PDA. If you believe that you are more efficient if you view and sort your e-mail only 5 times daily, you won't check your e-mail every time you have a break in the action. If you believe in keeping your inbox empty, you will empty it every time you open your e-mail.

Once you shift the way you think about e-mail, you can commit to changing the way you handle it.

So, what new beliefs will help you detoxify your inbox?

_____

_____

_____

164

SET GOALS

What are the specific e-mail handling goals that you want to achieve, and by when? In other words, if you were managing your e-mail optimally, what would your daily e-mail handling look like? How would your week work? Draw on the three assessments you've taken in this book. Write the five specific goals you'd like to achieve through Inbox Detox.

1. _____

   _____

2. _____

   _____

3. _____

   _____

4. _____

   _____

5. _____

   _____

EMBRACE THE TOOLS FOR CHANGE

No matter how committed and motivated you may be to make changes, you won't see lasting results unless you master the proper tools for changing your e-habits. This book provides you with a proven formula, practical help and

ー

guidance you need to Detox your Inbox. The tools for e-mail change are available, but it's up to you to embrace them in your daily routine, both at work and in your personal life.

So, what are the five specific tools or practices that will bring you the greatest return?

1. _____

_____

2. _____

_____

3. _____

_____

4. _____

_____

5. _____

_____

VALUE THE CHANGES

To help you clarify the importance of learning and embracing this program, it is helpful to try to quantify the value of the changes you intend to make. Sometimes these numbers can be astounding. If you can reclaim a half hour daily, what is that worth to you? If you can improve your career path, what is that worth to you? If you can reduce the number of e-mails you receive daily by 10, what is that worth to you?

So, take a moment now to quantify what these changes are worth to you:

_____

_____

_____

_____

_____

_____

FIND MOTIVATION

To make drastic changes in your habits, you must be motivated—after all, change takes time and effort. Find motivation for changing your e-habits in the results you expect to gain. What appeals most to you of all the results you will get out of better e-mail practices? More time to handle other tasks? Less spam? Better productivity and efficiency? Why do you want to change your e-mailing habits? Figure out the results that appeal to you and let them motivate you to change your habits. As politician Jim Ryun once said, "Motivation is what gets you started. Habit is what keeps you going."

So, what end results will motivate you to concentrate on changing your e-mailing habits?

_____

_____

_____

_____

_____

USE OBSTACLES

As with any forward progress, there may be obstacles. Take a moment now to write the obstacles that might derail your Inbox Detox success.

So, what are obstacles might block your achieving the goals you described?

_____

_____

_____

It is interesting to note that once you've identified obstacles, it becomes easier to overcome them.

So, what are the solutions to the obstacles you've noted?

_____

_____

_____

ANTICIPATE SETBACKS

No one is perfect, and we're not saying you need to aim for perfection. Let's go back to that dieter's example: he may slip and go for that chocolate cake at times, yet that doesn't mean that the entire diet is blown. Similarly, one slip-up in your e-mail practices doesn't justify giving up; be persistent and know that several weeks of focus are necessary to engrain the habits you want.

One of the participants called me about a month after a teleseminar, disappointed that he had not been able to keep his inbox zeroed out. When I asked how many items he had in his inbox, he said, "Twenty." I then asked him how many he had had prior to the teleseminar. "340," he replied. A noted improvement, I explained to him. It was then that he realized his success and congratulated himself on his progress, promising to sort those last twenty messages after we hung up.

Here is an e-mail I received after one of my e-mail productivity teleseminars. This person is obviously antici-pating the challenge of changing her habits:

169

> Thanks, Marsha,
>
> I am zeroed out! The folders are in place — now I just need the practiced self-discipline to "step away from the machine!"

Remember that small steps lead to large ones. Incremental progress is worth acknowledging, and can energize you to keep going.

So, how will you handle any setbacks in your e-mail handling?

_____

_____

_____

COMMIT TO LASTING CHANGE

No changes can last without a long-term commitment to make them last. You may purge your inbox the cleanest it has ever been, but if you fail to commit to keeping it clean, received e-mails will just pile up again, and your efforts at change will be all in vain. For lasting results, you must make a lasting commitment to changing your own e-mail habits and practices. Remember: the change starts with you!

So, what is the one most important result that you will have after you've engrained all these positive e-mailing practices?

_____

_____

_____

CELEBRATE

One of the most important things about achieving any goal is to celebrate. And incremental goals deserve celebrating, too. Planning for those celebrations can motivate you to continue on. Celebrate by doing something, no matter how small or large, but please celebrate each success along the way to Inbox Detox!

So, how are you going to celebrate each incremental achievement?

_____

_____

_____

THE ELATION

Here are words we've received from all over the world. Please share yours with us, too!

"My inbox is 'everclear!' I am actually managing my work!"

"I learned that I needed only to set up 4 new files in two different categories and suddenly, I was able to manage every single piece that was hanging in my growing in box."

"I created Priority A, B and C files; cleaned out my inbox; dumped by Delete File and deleted 5,475 sent messages. I feel at lot 'lighter' this morning, thanks to you."

"The folder split you recommended really makes sense and I've been clicking and dragging my little heart out."

"I am now a Wham Bam In Bin Emptying Machine."

"I'm excited to send this screen print of my empty inbox to you! My inbox is now empty and is going to stay that way!"

"I implemented your strategies last Friday, and although I felt guilty, now I feel much freer."

"Thank you from the bottom of my (very empty) in bin!"

"I heard a lot of comments about how great they thought a lot of the ideas were and how they couldn't believe all the bad habits they didn't know they had. My manager came out to me last week to show me that her Inbox was empty. Now the pressure is on for me to get mine cleaned up."

And, now that you've detoxified your inbox, and committed to the habit of e-mail excellence, how do you feel? Add your comment here, or share it with us at info@marshaegan.com.

LOOKING FORWARD

Wow! You have made it through the 12-step process. Your inbox is clean, and you are managing your workday by planning at a regularly scheduled times. Your action files are working, and you just love using the two-minute rule.

You've learned time saving and paper saving practices, and career blunders to avoid.

You have taken control of your e-mail instead of it controlling you. You've embraced e-mailing excellence and e-mailing etiquette as habits. Congratulations!

Your e-mail no longer controls you. Isn't that a great feeling? Some of my clients have actually said that through this process, they have taken back their lives. How about you?

As always,
To your success,

Marsha Egan

Order Form

Fax orders: Please send this form to 610-879-2073
Email orders: marsha@marshaegan.com
Online orders: http://InboxDetox.com/store

For our catalogue of other resources you can use, visit http://InboxDetox.com/store

If you would like to add any to your order, please place them on the order form.

Please send the following books, CDs, or reports. I understand that I may return any of them for full refund — for any reason, no questions asked.

_____

_____

Name: _____

Address: _____

City, State, Zip: _____

Telephone: _____

Email Address: _____

Number of books @ $19.95 _____

Shipping and Handling @ $3.00/book _____

PA Residents, 6% Sales Tax _____

Total _____

Payment by check: Check made payable to The Egan Group, Inc., 2 Seven Springs Drive, Reading, PA, 19607

Payment by Credit Card: Visa   MC   AMEX

Card Number: _____

Name on Card: _____ Exp. Date _____

Billing Address: _____

About The Author

Marsha Egan, PCC is an internationally recognized authority on e-mail productivity, having been featured on ABC Nightly News, Fox and Friends, Canada AM, and radio stations throughout the world, and had been interviewed in the Chicago Tribune,  Washington Post, New York Post, and countless other media outlets. She is president and CEO of The Egan Group, Inc., based in Reading, Pennsylvania. Named one of Pennsylvania's 50 Best Women in Business, she is a professional speaker and certified executive coach who specializes in helping clients regain productivity lost due to destructive work habits. You can visit her website at http://Inboxdetox.com for excellent resources that will help you reclaim your workday and your life. Contact Marsha at Marsha@MarshaEgan.com